SAT SMART
STRATEGY GUIDE

INCLUDES:

COLLEGE PLANNING STRATEGIES
for
NEW JERSEY STUDENTS

(STARTS ON PAGE 35)

ISBN-13: 978-1985754898
ISBN-10: 1985754894

SAT Smart
Signature Strategy Guide

STRUCTURE OF THE SAT EXAM

The length of the SAT is three hours, with the addition of a 50-minute optional essay. We highly recommend that students register for, and complete, the optional essay as it is required by many colleges.

The new SAT is comprised of five sections:

READING TEST: 65 minutes

Section 1 of the new SAT is the Reading Test. It is comprised of four single passages and one double passage. The reading selections cover three major subject areas: U.S. and World Literature, History/Social Studies, and Science. Some of the passages include selections from historical documents, such as the Declaration of Independence or the Constitution. Others contain graphs and charts that correlate to the passages. The passages range in length from 500 to 750 words. There are a total of 52 questions within a time frame of 65 minutes.

Writing and Language Test: 35 minutes

Section 2 of the new SAT is the Writing and Language Test. It is comprised of four passages in different subject areas, each of 400 to 450 words, of varying levels of complexity. One passage is a non-fiction narrative, one or two are informative/explanatory texts, and one or two are argumentative texts. This test measures students' skills in revising and editing texts with an emphasis on development, organization, and effective language use. There are a total of 44 questions (11 questions for each passage) within a time frame of 35 minutes.

Math Tests: 25 minutes and 55 minutes

There are two Math sections on the new SAT, sections 3 and 4. Section 3 does *not* allow the use of a calculator, while Section 4 does. Both sections present a table of formulas at the top of the section, reminding students of the formulas for the area and volume of geometric figures, the circumference of a circle, the proportions of special right triangles, the Pythagorean Theorem, and three key facts:

The number of degrees of arc in a circle is 360.
The number of radians of arc in a circle is 2π.
The sum of the measures in degrees of the angles of a triangle is 180.

The four areas of concentration on the Math sections of the new SAT are:

1) Heart of Algebra: Comprises 33% of Math problems with 19 questions.
Focuses on linear equations and systems of linear equations

2) Problem Solving and Data Analysis: Comprises 29% of Math problems with 17 questions
Focuses on ratios, percentages, proportional reasoning, and the analysis of graphs and statistical data

3) Passport to Advanced Math: Comprises 28% of Math problems with 16 questions
Focuses on more complex equations and functions and includes geometry, trigonometry, radian measure, and the computation of complex numbers

4) Additional Topics in Math: Comprises 10% of Math problems with 6 questions
Focuses on area and volume calculations, theorems with lines, angles, triangles and circles, and problems with trigonometric functions

Math Test (No Calculator): 25 minutes

Section 3 of the new SAT consists of 20 Math questions that must be solved without the use of a calculator. This section consists of 15 multiple choice questions as well as 5 open-ended questions whereby students must solve and then grid-in their answers.

Math Test (Calculator allowed): 55 minutes

Section 4 of the new SAT consists of 38 questions and allows the use of a calculator. The first 30 are multiple choice questions, while the last 8 are open-ended questions which students must solve and then grid-in their answers. Students may use a calculator of choice, including a graphing calculator that is helpful, but not essential, in solving several problems. Students who are not comfortable with a graphing calculator should use a scientific calculator.

Students are not provided with scrap paper for any section of the SAT, including the two Math sections, but are allowed to write in their test booklet. It is particularly helpful for students, when working on the Math questions, to draw diagrams, fill in the measures of geometric figures, and write down any helpful information or computations while working on each problem.

Essay (Optional): 50 minutes

Although the essay is optional, it should be written by each student taking the new SAT as it is required by many colleges that use SAT scores as a criterion for admission and/or scholarships. The essay section presents a passage of 650 to 750 words in length that examines ideas, trends and debatable issues drawn from the arts, sciences, civic, cultural, and political life. Students are asked *not* to focus on whether or not they agree with the argument presented in the passage, but rather to analyze how the author builds a persuasive argument. Students are given four lined pages on which to write their essay.

SCORING THE SAT

The SAT is scored on a range of 200 to 800 points in each of two areas:

Evidence-Based Reading and Writing – a scoring chart converts the points earned on the Reading Test to a sub-score (in the range of 10-40) and the points earned on the Writing and Language Test to a sub-score (in the range of 10-40). These two sub-scores are added together and then multiplied by 10, giving each student an Evidence-Based Reading and Writing score in the range of 200 to 800. In order for a student to earn a median score of 500, he/she needs to correctly answer approximately 48 of the 96 questions correctly on a combination of these two sections.

Math – a scoring chart converts the total number of points earned on a combination of the two Math tests to a score in the range of 200 to 800. In order for a student to earn a median math score of 500, he/she needs to correctly answer approximately 26 of the 58 questions on Sections 3 and 4 of the SAT.

A student receives one point for every correct answer on the SAT. There is no penalty for incorrect answers, so students should always guess rather than leave a question blank. Easy questions count just as much as hard questions, so students should not spend too much time on any one question. Rather, it is best to skip any questions that are particularly difficult and return to them later, if time allows. When the allotted time for a section is nearing, students should guess on any questions that remain unanswered. Since there are four choices (A to D) for each multiple-choice question, random guessing provides a 25% chance of choosing the correct answer!

The Essay is scored separately, and does not impact the Evidence-Based Reading and Writing Score. Two readers score each essay, assigning a score in the range of 1 to 4 in each of three areas. Their scores are added together, giving each essay a score in the range of 2 to 8 for each of the three areas. These areas are:

Reading – How well a student demonstrates an understanding of the passage

Analysis – The effectiveness of explaining how the author builds his/her argument

Writing – The cohesiveness of the essay, effective use of language, ability to convey central and supporting claims or ideas, a recognizable introduction and conclusion, varied sentence structure, precise word choice, and a strong command of the conventions of standard written English.

Students are allotted 50 minutes to read a passage of 650-750 words and write an essay analyzing how the author builds a persuasive argument. Students are provided with four lined pages on which to write an essay.

Recommendations

* Be thoroughly familiar with the format and content of the new SAT. It is *not a secret* what the new test looks like or what material is covered on each section!

* Be thoroughly familiar with the directions for each test section. By knowing, and understanding, the directions for each test section in advance, students can use all of the allotted time to earn points and not use it to figure out what they need to do. This is particularly helpful for the Math grid-in questions!

* Understand how the test is scored. For all test questions, students earn one point for each correct answer. There is not a point deduction for incorrect answers, so students should guess when in doubt. Since most test questions are multiple-choice with four options (A, B, C and D), even totally random guessing will provide correct answers approximately 25% of the time! Ideally, when students are unsure of an answer they should try to narrow down their choices by crossing out answers they believe are incorrect and then picking from the potential answers that they have remaining.

* Understand the grading rubric for the essay, noting that you are not being asked to agree or disagree with the author's position but rather to analyze how effectively the argument was presented.

READING TEST
(65 minutes, 52 questions)

The first section of the SAT exam is the Reading Test which, at 65 minutes, is the longest section of the exam. It is strictly a test of reading comprehension as it is comprised of four single passages and one double passage, each followed by a series of ten or eleven questions. The passages vary both in subject matter and in levels of complexity.

The reading passages address a wide range of topics including U.S. and World Literature, History and Social Studies, and an assortment of issues in the field of Science. It is important for students to realize that they are not expected to use any prior knowledge to aid them in answering questions. All answers should be chosen based strictly on information explicitly stated, or implied, in the passages.

The passages on the Reading Test vary greatly in their level of difficulty. Some passages are on par with the critical reading skills expected of students in their first two years of high school, while other passages are based on the abilities expected of students in college-level courses. The length of each passage is typically between 500 and 750 words.

SAT Smart Reading Test
Signature Strategies

1. Students should read the passages in the order in which they appear on the test. Since there are ten or eleven questions based on each passage, it is not an option to skip a passage. So students should *not* waste time by skipping around and doing the passage on their favorite topic first.

2. Likewise, students should *not* skip around among the questions. They should read each passage in its entirety, and then refer back to the passage as they answer each question. The questions following each passage are not arranged in order of difficulty. The overall questions about the central idea, theme, and author's point of view, tend to appear first. These questions often start with phrases such as, "The passage most strongly suggests that..." or "The central claim of the passage is that..."

3. Students should be especially careful when answering the subsequent, more specific "duo" questions, which often focus on the ways in which the author supports a point of view. Students are often asked to draw a reasonable conclusion or inference from a passage and then, in a follow-up question, to identify the specific textual evidence in the passage that leads to the conclusion or inference. Two points are at stake here. It is important for students to carefully focus on the first of these questions, because if it is answered incorrectly there is little likelihood of answering the partner question correctly. Once the first of the duo questions is answered, students should refer back to the passage to consider each of the lines referenced in choices A through D and choose the one that supports the answer to the prior question.

4. There are several "vocabulary in context" questions where students are given a specific line in the passage to refer back to and asked what a particular word means. The best way to answer such a question is to go back to the referenced line in the passage and try to think of an appropriate word that could be used as a substitute. Then, look at choices A, B, C and D and choose the one closest in meaning to the substitute word.

For example, consider a sentence in a passage that states, "The professor feared that the university's new policy of marking tests on a curve conveyed a lessening of expectations on the part of its students." A question might read, "As used in line 29, *conveyed* most nearly means....." The choices might be:

A) delivered
B) transported
C) communicated
D) carried

If a student read the sentence above and tried to substitute an appropriate word for "conveyed," he/she might think of "expressed." When looking at the four multiple-choice options, the student should recognize that "communicated" is the closest in meaning to "expressed."

5. There will be at least one passage on the Reading Test that contains a graph or chart that correlates to the passage. Students should not spend time analyzing the graph or chart until they come to a specific question focusing on it. Usually, the question will ask students to identify information that is clearly portrayed. Students should not be intimidated or anticipate that questions based on the graph or chart will be particularly complex.

6. There is always a *double passage* on the Reading Test. Passage 1 and Passage 2 will be on similar topics, but with differing perspectives. The double passage will be followed by some questions focusing specifically on Passage 1, and other questions concentrating on Passage 2. There will also be questions asking students to compare the viewpoints, central ideas, themes, textual evidence, and main conclusions between the two passages. Students should read Passage 1 first and then answer the beginning questions based solely on this passage. Then, students should read Passage 2 and likewise answer the next questions specific to that passage. Finally, students should answer the remaining, comparison questions.

7. Students should be sure to fill in an answer for each question, even if they are taking an educated guess. No answer should ever be left blank, as there is not a "wrong answer penalty." Since there are four possible answer choices for each question, even random guessing will, according to the Laws of Probability, result in a correct answer, earning one point, 25% of the time. When students are struggling to find the correct answer, they should put a line through the letter (A, B, C or D) of any answer they believe to be incorrect and then take a *good guess* and move on! Students will get credit if they are correct and, if they are wrong, it is no worse than having left the answer blank.

In order to avoid being overwhelmed by the number of passages and seemingly complex questions they will face on the Reading Test, students should be sure to do practice tests well in advance of their actual test day. It takes practice to be able to read each passage carefully, while working at a pace that will allow for the successful completion of 52 questions within the 65 minute time frame.

WRITING AND LANGUAGE TEST
(35 minutes, 44 questions)

The second section of the SAT exam is the Writing and Language Test which, at 35 minutes, is one of the shorter sections of the exam. This section is comprised of four "stories," each followed by 11 questions. The stories, or passages, are typically between 400 and 450 words and are in different subject areas with varying levels of complexity. One passage is a non-fiction narrative, one or two are informative/ explanatory texts, and one or two are argumentative texts. The Writing and Language Test measures a student's skills in revising and editing texts with an emphasis on development, organization, and effective language use. There are a total of 44 questions to be answered within a time frame of 35 minutes.

Some questions pertain to a specific underlined section of a story and students are asked to identify errors in sentence structure, usage or punctuation. Other questions isolate a paragraph and ask, for example, where a specific sentence should be placed or if a certain sentence should be added or deleted. There are also questions focused on the meaning of the story in its entirety.

The Writing and Language Test typically contains one story with a chart, graph or table. Students need to analyze the information presented in this material in order to correct one or more sentences in the passage. There are also several "vocabulary" questions in which students are given the option to replace a specific word in a story with any of three other words.

To give an example of a typical passage, and the type of questions that students can expect, we have excerpted an article that was published in the Courier News and online at www.SATsmart.com, written by SAT Smart director Susan Alaimo. It typifies the questions that students will face on a passage in the Writing and Language Test.

Comfortable Lifestyle at College

Picture a residence with private bedrooms and bathrooms, walk-in closets, a washer and dryer in each unit, and fully equipped kitchens (including a Keurig coffee machine). Step outside to the rooftop infinity pool, a 22 foot LED TV, a grilling gazebo, hammocks, and a sand volleyball court — with stadium seating. If you **1** <u>envisioned</u> a five star resort, it's quite understandable. But this is actually the description of living quarters being enjoyed by some students attending the University of Arizona in Tucson.

College living is not what it used to be. Certainly, there are still colleges with drab dormitories featuring a bathroom at each end of the hallway to be shared by scores of students. **2** <u>Likewise</u> more and more colleges are realizing that a key strategy for attracting students used to the comforts of home is to offer more luxurious amenities than they would expect.

At the University of North Florida in Jacksonville, a lazy river is a welcome addition to the tennis, volleyball, and basketball courts. **3** <u>Other recreational amenities are a putting green and a lighted running track.</u> The University of Florida in Gainesville boasts a residence hall with a sun deck, private jetted Jacuzzis, living rooms with fireplaces and big screen televisions, and gourmet kitchens.

Washington University in St. Louis, Missouri focuses on sleeping comfort with Tempur-Pedic beds featured in a residence hall **4** <u>that hosts a rooftop garden, a fitness center complete with a dance studio, a bakery,</u> and a separate kosher kitchen with a full menu. The University of Texas in Austin offers fully furnished apartments with leather couches, stainless steel appliances and hardwood floors — and maid service to keep everything clean!

One of the most unusual amenities **5** <u>was offered by</u> <u>MIT</u> (Massachusetts Institute of Technology). Its Simmons Hall residence, often referred to as The Sponge for its unique exterior, hosts a giant ball pit where students can work off their stresses. Afterwards, they can enjoy refreshing drinks from their campus eatery that won the World Smoothie Award five times!

6 <u>It's going to be tough for students to return home for</u> <u>semester breaks!</u>

QUESTIONS:

1
(A) NO CHANGE
(B) are envisioning
(C) were envisioning
(D) wanted to envision

2
(A) NO CHANGE
(B) But
(C) In addition
(D) Therefore

3
The writer is considering deleting the underlined sentence. Should the writer do this?
(A) Yes, the point has already been made in the previous sentence.
(B) Yes, it's irrelevant to the main point of the passage.
(C) No, it provides further information in support of the main point of the passage.
(D) No, it offers the most important evidence in the passage.

4

(A) NO CHANGE
(B) that hosts a rooftop garden; a fitness center complete
    with a dance studio; a bakery;
(C) that hosts a rooftop garden: a fitness center complete
    with a dance studio: a bakery:
(D) that hosts a rooftop garden - a fitness center
    complete with a dance studio - a bakery -

5

(A) NO CHANGE
(B) happened at MIT
(C) used to be offered at MIT
(D) is offered at MIT

6

Which choice best maintains the tone established in the passage?
(A) NO CHANGE
(B) Not all college students live like this.
(C) Parents are often surprised when they tour colleges.
(D) Students work hard and deserve to play hard.

Answer Key: 1. (B) 2. (B) 3. (C) 4. (A) 5. (D) 6. (A)

SAT Smart Writing and Language Test Signature Strategies

1. Read through each passage carefully and methodically. Do not skip paragraphs that do not have questions based on them, as you will need to comprehend the overall message of each passage in order to answer general questions.

2. Note that the numbers in parentheses but NOT in bold represent the sentence numbers, while the numbers in black boxes represent the question numbers.

3. Consider the four answer options (one of which will typically be "no change") for each question, as it's often quickest to eliminate the poor choices and back into the correct answer.

4. For questions asking whether a certain sentence should be added or deleted, first decide on a "no" or "yes" answer, thus reducing your options to two possibilities, and then choose the answer that gives the best rationale for your choice.

5. Carefully examine each sentence for the correct tense, structure, word choice and punctuation when choosing an answer.

6. Answer each question as you work your way through each story, as there is not a penalty for wrong answers. Circle the question number in your test book if you are guessing, and go back and reconsider your answer later if time allows.

MATH TESTS
Section 3 (25 minutes, 20 questions)
Section 4 (55 minutes, 38 questions)

The third and fourth sections of the SAT exam comprise the Math Test. Section 3 does *not* allow the use of a calculator, while Section 4 does. Both sections present a table of formulas at the top of the section, reminding students of the following formulas:

Area of a circle = πr^2
Circumference of a circle = $2\pi r$
Area of a rectangle = length • width
Area of a triangle = ½ • base • height
Pythagorean theorem: $c^2 = a^2 + b^2$
The proportion of side measurements of a 30 – 60 – 90 degree right triangle is, respectively: x, x√3, 2x
The proportion of side measurements of a 45 – 45 – 90 degree right triangle is, respectively: s, s, s√2
Volume of a rectangular solid = length • width • height
Volume of a cylindrical solid = πr^2 • height
Volume of a sphere = $4/3\pi r^3$
Volume of a cone = $1/3\pi r^2$ • height
Volume of a pyramid = 1/3 • length • width • height

Students also need to know:
The number of degrees of arc in a circle is 360.
The number of radians of arc in a circle is 2π.
The sum of the measures in degrees of the angles of a triangle is 180.

There are four specific areas of Math that are the focus of the Math sections of the redesigned SAT exam. They are:

1) Heart of Algebra – focuses on the ability to analyze and create linear equations, inequalities, and functions. Some questions involve straightforward "problem solving" situations, others require interpreting the relationship between graphical and algebraic

representations, while others require mastery of absolute value expressions, inequalities and equations.

2) Problem Solving and Data Analysis – includes ratios, percentages, and proportional reasoning in problem solving situations. This section also includes analyzing graphs, charts, tables and scatterplots.

3) Passport to Advanced Math – requires work with expressions involving exponentials, integer and rational powers, radicals, or fractions with a variable in the denominator. Questions deal with polynomials, quadratic functions and equations, and the relationships between algebraic and graphical representations of functions.

4) Additional Topics in Math – calculating area and volume, using theorems to solve problems with lines, angles, triangles and circles, and working with trigonometric functions.

Each of the two Math sections starts with multiple-choice questions which increase in difficulty from easy to hard. There are four multiple-choice options offered for each question. Students should use their test booklet to work through calculations, as scrap paper is not provided. Students should draw diagrams, label angles, and make each question as visual as possible. Do not rely on mental math, as it is easy to make "careless" mistakes under the pressure of a timed exam. When allowed, always use a calculator, even for simple calculations.

When struggling with a question, try to narrow down the choices and then back into the correct answer. For example, if asked to identify the slope of a graph, the question will typically give two answer choices with a positive slope and two answer choices with a negative slope. Most students, by simply looking at the graph, can identify whether the line is moving up (positive slope) or down (negative slope) as it goes from left to right. This will narrow down the potentially correct answer to two choices, making it easier for the student to solve. At this point, even random guessing will provide a 50% chance of earning credit.

Each of the two math sections concludes with open-ended questions. Students must come up with their own answer (as opposed to selecting from four multiple-choice options) and then properly *bubble in* the answer. Students should be thoroughly familiar with the instructions for recording their answers well in advance of their test day, so they do not waste precious time figuring out the proper procedure. Students are given four column boxes in which to record their answers. They are instructed to use as many columns as necessary to properly record their answers. It is acceptable to record an answer as a fraction or a decimal. For example, if students want to record the answer 1½, they have two options. They can record it as a decimal, which would read .5, or they can record it as a fraction, which would read *3/2*. Note that students *should not* record the answer *one and a half* as *11/2* since that would be interpreted as eleven halves. Students should note that the correct answer will never be a negative number as there is no way to record a negative answer. There may be questions with more than one correct answer, in which case students simply grid in *one* correct answer.

SAT Smart Math Test
Signature Strategies

1. Students should work through the questions in sequential order, working at a steady pace but not too quickly to sacrifice accuracy. The multiple-choice questions increase in difficulty as students move through the section, and the grid-in questions do the same. When students come upon a question that they do not know how to do, or one that will require a substantial amount of time to solve, they should circle the question number in their test booklet (to remind themselves that they guessed) and then bubble in an answer – even if it is a random guess. There is no deduction for wrong answers, so students should *always* fill in an answer. The Laws of Probability predict that, when there are four possible answers, random guessing will provide a correct choice one out of four times! If students have time left over at the end of their section, they can go back and reconsider the circled questions on which they guessed.

2. Students should use their test booklet as scrap paper, as none will be provided. The test booklet is not sacred, and can be written all over. There are many Math questions that become much easier to solve when students draw a diagram, or label the sides and angles of one that is provided. Students should solve problems on their test paper, making each problem as visual as possible and working through each one step-by-step.

3. On Section 4, where the use of a calculator is allowed, students should use one even for simple calculations, as it is easy to make mistakes under the pressure of a timed exam. Students should be sure to bring a calculator that is approved for use on the SAT. Most graphing calculators, and all

scientific calculators, are approved. Students can see the list of approved calculators at: sat.collegeboard.org/register/calculator-policy

4. Students should familiarize themselves with the test directions ahead of time so they can maximize the amount of time they have to actually solve problems. This is particularly important for the open-ended questions where there is an entire page of directions explaining how the answers need to be bubbled in to receive credit.

5. Students should remember to refer to the box of formulas that will appear at the beginning of each Math section. When using these formulas, students should look at the multiple-choice answer options to see in what form they want the answer. For example, when asked to calculate the area of a circle, students usually need to leave the answer in terms of π and not multiply it by 3.14.

6. Although most of the math formulas that students need to know are provided in a box at the beginning of each math section, there are two that are not. Students should know the center-radius form of the circle equation: $(x - h)^2 + (y - k)^2 = r^2$ with the center being at point (h, k) and the radius being "r". Students should also know the following quadratic formulas: $ax^2 + bx + c = 0$ and $x = -b \pm \sqrt{b^2 - 4ac} / 2a$

7. Practice, practice, and then practice some more! The same types of problems are asked over and over again on the SAT. By doing actual practice test sections, using material provided by The College Board, students will become familiar with the types of questions they will face on the real test and comfortable working within the allotted time frame.

ESSAY
(50 minutes)

The last section of the SAT exam is the optional essay. While students are not required to register for, and complete, this section, it is advisable that they do so as the essay is required by many colleges. The essay section requires students to read a passage that typically ranges from 650 to 750 words, and then write an essay explaining how the author builds a persuasive argument.

It's important for students to realize that they are *not* being asked to agree or disagree with the author's point of view. Rather, they are being asked to analyze how the author develops the argument. Students should consider, for example, whether the author cites evidence, uses reasoning to develop ideas and to connect claims and evidence, and/or appeals to emotion.

Students are provided with four lined pages on which to write their essay, and a planning page at the front of their answer booklet on which to jot down notes or outline their essay. It is vital that students stick to the topic and use a regular # 2 (not mechanical) pencil.

Students should read through the passage very carefully and underline, as they read, any sentences or phrases that they feel contribute to the persuasive argument being made by the author. In the margins, next to each underlined section, students should note the "strategy" the author is using in developing the persuasive nature of the passage.

Once students have finished reading the entire passage, they should write their introductory paragraph with an opening sentence stating that the author wrote an extremely persuasive essay/story/letter about (name the topic). Students should then elaborate, throughout the rest of the opening paragraph, on the "strategies" used by the author that they had noted in the margins.

Students should then write a separate body paragraph for each persuasive strategy, quoting directly from the passage and elaborating on why it was effective. Students should be sure to allow time and space to write a solid concluding paragraph. Here, students should summarize the strategies used in the passage and reiterate that the author presented a powerful case for (name the topic).

SAT Smart Essay
Signature Strategies

1. Students should expect that the essay prompt will remain the same from one SAT test to the next; only the passage will change. Students need to remember that they are not being asked to agree or disagree with the author's point of view. Rather, they are required to write an essay analyzing the author's techniques and effectiveness in developing a persuasiveness argument.

2. Students should read through the passage slowly and deliberately, underlining areas that contribute to the persuasive nature of the passage. In the margin, next to each underlined area, students should write notes indicating the technique used to develop a persuasive argument. (e.g. "appeals to emotion," or "establishes credibility," or "presents counter-argument and effectively refutes it."

3. Students should then write an introductory paragraph (utilizing the margin notes) stating the techniques used by the author in developing the persuasive nature of the passage. The subsequent body paragraphs should each cite an example of a method used and refer back to the passage to provide examples (drawn from the underlined phrases). Students should be sure to write a concluding paragraph summarizing the author's effectiveness in presenting a persuasive argument and referring to the techniques used to support the author's argument.

4. Students should allow time to proofread their essay, inserting editing marks where necessary and correcting any spelling or grammatical errors.

5. Students must stay on topic, use a regular #2 (not mechanical) pencil, and write legibly while staying within the margins of the pages.

6. The Essay is scored separately, and does not impact the Evidence-based Reading & Writing score. Two readers each score the essay, assigning a score in the range of 1 to 4 in each of three areas: Reading, Analysis, and Writing. The scores are added together, giving the student a score in the range of 2 to 8 in each of the three areas.

Circle answers below: Section 1 Reading Test
You will be bubbling in answers on the actual SAT.

1. A B C (D)
2. A (B) C D
3. A (B) C D
4. A B (C) D
5. A B (C) D
6. (A) B C D
7. A B (C) D
8. A B (C) D
9. A (B) C D
10. A B (C) D
11. A B C (D)
12. A B C (D)
13. A B C (D)
14. A (B) C D
15. A B (C) D
16. A B (C) D
17. (A) B C D

18. (A) B C D
19. A B (C) D
20. A (B) C D
21. A B C (D)
22. A (B) C D
23. A B C (D)
24. A (B) C D
25. A B C (D)
26. A (B) C D
27. (A) B C D
28. (A) B C D
29. A B (C) D
30. A (B) C D
31. A B (C) D
32. A B C (D)
33. A B (C) D
34. A (B) C D

35. (A) B C D
36. A (B) C D
37. A B (C) D
38. A B C (D)
39. A (B) C D
40. A (B) C D
41. (A) B C D
42. A B (C) D
43. (A) B C D
44. A (B) C D
45. A B (C) D
46. A B C (D)
47. A B C (D)
48. A (B) C D
49. (A) B C D
50. A B (C) D
51. A (B) C D
52. (A) B C D

Write the number of questions you answered correctly: 35

To calculate your Reading score, find the number of questions you answered correctly and circle your SAT Reading Score.

1. 100	18. 210	35. 300
2. 100	19. 220	36. 310
3. 110	20. 220	37. 310
4. 120	21. 230	38. 320
5. 130	22. 230	39. 320
6. 140	23. 240	40. 330
7. 150	24. 240	41. 330
8. 150	25. 250	42. 340
9. 160	26. 250	43. 350
10. 170	27. 260	44. 350
11. 170	28. 260	45. 360
12. 180	29. 270	46. 370
13. 190	30. 280	47. 370
14. 190	31. 280	48. 380
15. 200	32. 290	49. 380
16. 200	33. 290	50. 390
17. 210	34. 300	51. 400
		52. 400

Circle answers below: Section 2 Writing & Language Test
You will be bubbling in answers on the actual SAT.

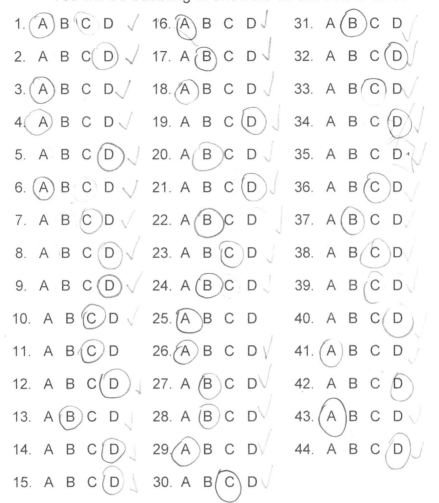

1. (A) B C D ✓   16. (A) B C D ✓   31. A (B) C D ✓
2. A B C (D) ✓   17. A (B) C D ✓   32. A B C (D) ✓
3. (A) B C D ✓   18. (A) B C D ✓   33. A B (C) D ✓
4. (A) B C D ✓   19. A B C (D) ✓   34. A B C (D) ✓
5. A B C (D) ✓   20. A (B) C D ✓   35. A B C D ✓
6. (A) B C D ✓   21. A B C (D) ✓   36. A B (C) D ✓
7. A B (C) D ✓   22. A (B) C D ✓   37. A (B) C D ✓
8. A B C (D) ✓   23. A B (C) D ✓   38. A B (C) D ✓
9. A B C (D) ✓   24. A (B) C D ✓   39. A B (C) D ✓
10. A B (C) D ✓   25. (A) B C D   40. A B C (D) ✓
11. A B (C) D   26. (A) B C D ✓   41. (A) B C D ✓
12. A B C (D) ✓   27. A (B) C D ✓   42. A B C (D)
13. A (B) C D ✓   28. A (B) C D ✓   43. (A) B C D ✓
14. A B C (D) ✓   29. (A) B C D ✓   44. A B C (D) ✓
15. A B C (D) ✓   30. A B (C) D ✓

Write the number of questions you answered correctly: 34

29

To calculate your Writing & Language score, find the number of questions you answered correctly and circle your SAT Writing & Language Score

1. 100	16. 200	31. 300
2. 100	17. 210	32. 300
3. 100	18. 210	33. 310
4. 110	19. 220	34. 320
5. 120	20. 230	35. 320
6. 130	21. 230	36. 330
7. 130	22. 240	37. 340
8. 140	23. 250	38. 340
9. 150	24. 250	39. 350
10. 160	25. 260	40. 360
11. 160	26. 260	41. 370
12. 170	27. 270	42. 380
13. 180	28. 280	43. 390
14. 190	29. 280	44. 400
15. 190	30. 290	

Reading Score 300 + Writing & Language Score 320 =

Evidence-based Reading & Writing Score 620
(Range: 200 - 800)

Circle or write answers below: Section 3 Math

You will be bubbling in answers on the actual SAT.

1. A B C D

2. (A) B C D

3. A B C (D)

4. (A) B C D

5. A B (C) D

6. A (B) C D

7. A (B) C D

8. A B C (D)

9. A B C (D)

10. A B (C) D

11. A B C (D)

12. A (B) C D

13. A B (C) D

14. A B C (D)

15. (A) B C D

16. 360 cm^3.

17. 2

18. -2

19. _____ ?

20. 3

Write the number of questions you answered correctly: _____

Circle or write answers below: Section 4 Math
You will be bubbling in answers on the actual SAT.

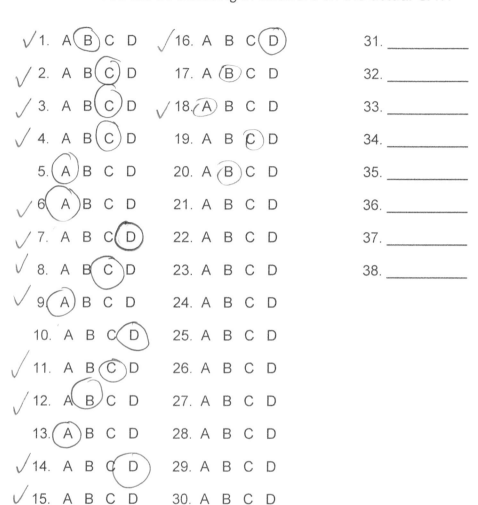

✓1. A (B) C D   ✓16. A B C (D)   31. _____

✓2. A B (C) D   17. A (B) C D   32. _____

✓3. A B (C) D   ✓18. (A) B C D   33. _____

✓4. A B (C) D   19. A B (C) D   34. _____

5. (A) B C D   20. A (B) C D   35. _____

✓6. (A) B C D   21. A B C D   36. _____

✓7. A B C (D)   22. A B C D   37. _____

✓8. A B (C) D   23. A B C D   38. _____

✓9. (A) B C D   24. A B C D

10. A B C (D)   25. A B C D

✓11. A B (C) D   26. A B C D

✓12. A (B) C D   27. A B C D

13. (A) B C D   28. A B C D

✓14. A B C (D)   29. A B C D

✓15. A B C D   30. A B C D

Write the number of questions you answered correctly: 14

To calculate your Math score, add together your total number of correct answers for Sections 3 & 4 and find your corresponding Math SAT Score below.
(Range: 200 – 800)

1. 200	21. 460	41. 620
2. 210	22. 470	42. 630
3. 230	23. 480	43. 640
4. 240	24. 480	44. 650
5. 260	25. 490	45. 660
6. 280	26. 500	46. 670
7. 290	27. 510	47. 670
8. 310	28. 520	48. 680
9. 320	29. 520	49. 690
10. 330	30. 530	50. 700
11. 340	31. 540	51. 710
12. 360	32. 550	52. 730
13. 370	33. 560	53. 740
14. 380	34. 560	54. 750
15. 390	35. 570	55. 760
16. 410	36. 580	56. 780
17. 420	37. 590	57. 790
18. 430	38. 600	58. 800
19. 440	39. 600	
20. 450	40. 610	

Evidence-based Reading & Writing score:
_____
(Range: 200 - 800)

+

Math Score: _____
(Range: 200- 800)

=

Total SAT Score: _____
(Range: 400 – 1600)

College Planning Strategies
for
New Jersey Students

By Susan Alaimo

College Planning Strategies
for New Jersey Students

There's so much information that *all* college-bound students need to think about, starting in their freshman year of high school. They need to begin identifying their areas of passion and pursuing clubs, activities, internships, and experiences that will demonstrate a level of knowledge and commitment once their senior year rolls around. They need to establish a pattern of involvement in volunteer work that, ideally, is compatible with their areas of passion. They need to choose courses as "electives" that may help them identify, or rule out, potential college majors. What students do during their first three years of high school will greatly impact the strength of the college applications they will file early in their senior year.

Many of the college preparation experiences of New Jersey high school students are exactly the same as those of students throughout the country – such as striving for the best grades and preparing for, and taking, SAT or ACT exams. But there is much information, specific to New Jersey students, that is particularly invaluable to them. New Jersey college-bound students would do well to learn from the experiences of their peers who preceded them. There are more than 3,000 colleges and universities in the U.S., and no one is able to research and/or visit them all. So it's extremely beneficial to find out which colleges are most popular with New Jersey students over the course of recent years. (Hint: New Jersey students who leave the state for college head, in the largest numbers, to the University of Delaware, Penn State, Drexel, and NYU.

In addition, many states have scholarship programs that are available solely to their residents. Only New Jersey students, for example, are eligible for the NJ Stars scholarship program that covers the cost of tuition at the state's 19 community colleges and then provides funds for students who move on to public four-year colleges and universities. Only New Jersey students are eligible for a vast array of academic, merit, and/or need-based scholarships: Governor's Urban Scholarship Program, Woodrow Wilson New Jersey Teaching Fellowship, NJSCPA (New Jersey Society of Certified Public Accountants) High School Scholarship, and the New Jersey State Golf Association Caddie Scholarships.

This guide provides New Jersey students with the strategies, opportunities, and information they need to consider as they navigate the fascinating, yet sometimes overwhelming, path towards a successful college search.

TABLE OF CONTENTS

IV. Filing Successful College Applications

V. Finances, Scholarships, Avoiding College Debt

Part I. The Early Years (of High School)

The Importance of Volunteer Work

One quality that college admissions people particularly value in applicants is a commitment to volunteer work. Colleges are impressed with students who have demonstrated a long-term commitment to a cause or organization that is important to them. Not everyone has to volunteer at a hospital, although that's a great activity for students seeking a career in the medical profession. The key is for students, early in their high school years, to identify a cause they are passionate about and then get involved to truly make an impact.

Students who have not yet become engaged in "giving back" can likely find an activity of interest on the Jersey Cares website (www.jerseycares.org) which features activities to suit almost any personality. *Pet Playground* offers the opportunity to work at animal adoption events. *Earth Keeper* volunteers work to beautify parks, gardens and green spaces throughout New Jersey. *Chess for Success* volunteers teach children the higher-level thinking and social skills utilized in this challenging game.

There are often so many volunteer opportunities right in a student's backyard. Athletes might cherish the opportunity to coach students - in basketball, football, tennis, or soccer - through their town's recreation program. Or, volunteer at the local YMCA or get involved with New Jersey Special Olympics, headquartered in Lawrenceville, NJ. Girl Scouts or Boy Scouts can choose to mentor a younger troop in their community. Dancers can offer free lessons in their area of specialty – Irish Step Dancing, Indian Dance, or Jazz – to students at afterschool centers.

Students looking to spread their wings often find that volunteer work provides a great opportunity to travel cheaply while doing some good. Ideally, students should choose to visit a part of the world that fascinates them and a type of volunteer work that coincides with their interests and potential life work.

The travel-abroad site *GoOverseas.com* offers students the chance to read about hundreds of programs, ask questions of travelers who have been there, and apply to programs of interest. The choice of locations is vast. Students can choose from over 100 countries, from those with which they are likely familiar (France, Germany, Italy, Spain, Switzerland) to those that may not be on their radar (Benin, Cameroon, Malawi, Myanmar, Vanatu).

The opportunities are almost limitless. Volunteer programs are offered in a wide variety of fields, including elephant, primate or sea turtle conservation, orphan, elderly, or disabled care, computer literacy, refugee or disaster relief, women's rights, reforestation, veterinary service, education, agriculture, business, teaching, tourism, and many more. In reality, it would be difficult for a student not to find an area of interest.

Although there are volunteer opportunities abroad at any time of year, there are many that exclusively run during the summer. For example, students can live in beautiful Tenerife, Spain and work with the island's threatened whale and dolphin populations. Or, students can choose to live with host families outside of Zambia, Africa and teach local students, work with orphans, help out at hospitals, or participate in construction projects. Volunteers seeking a chance to see the wildlife, beaches, historical sites and mountains in the Andes, Peru, can work in the heart of the Amazon on a rainforest conservation program.

DoSomething.org, one of the largest U.S. organizations helping teens get involved in causes they care about, released a study tying volunteerism to college admissions. The results indicate that admissions officers place a high value on a student's long-term commitment to a cause or organization. Consistency is the priority, as colleges prefer students who support one cause over a period of time, demonstrating commitment and perseverance.

Colleges favor students with a history of volunteerism with the hope that their commitment will enrich the college community, where there are limitless opportunities for involvement. Rutgers University hosts about 50 student organizations that focus on community service initiatives in areas including affordable housing, animal care, mental health advocacy and international and social justice.

The College of New Jersey offers between 50 to 100 percent tuition scholarships to students who make a substantial commitment to volunteerism by becoming Bonner Community Scholars. These students choose to focus on one area of service, such as hunger, homelessness, the environment, juvenile justice, immigrant services or urban education, and provide 300 hours of meaningful service over the course of a year, combining service with their academic experiences.

Aside from its boost to their college applications, volunteerism is extremely beneficial to students in so many ways. It tends to make them aware, and grateful, for the many blessings of their lives. It empowers young people to realize that they can make a difference in the world. It helps them put their priorities in order and use their time productively. It helps students develop vital skills, such as working collaboratively with others towards a mutual goal. It often has the surprising affect of helping students identify their life calling, and with it their college major!

Showcasing a Unique Talent

Years ago, college-bound students were advised to present themselves as well-rounded individuals on their college applications. So, while in high school, they would join a gamut of activities, ranging from sports to music to academic-oriented clubs such as debate teams and Model U.N. Those days are long gone. Colleges are no longer looking for renaissance students who have spread themselves thin, engaged in many activities. Rather, colleges are seeking students with a particular passion and expertise that they have developed over the course of time. Colleges are seeking depth over breadth, so students should choose wisely.

Colleges, particularly the most selective institutions, are seeking students with a distinctive quality, accomplishment or talent – in almost any arena. By bringing to their campus thousands of highly accomplished students they are able to successfully create an impressive and vibrant environment.

Students of all ages should try to identify their passion, and then devote their time and efforts to becoming the very best they can be. If athletics is their choice, it's a good idea to keep in mind some of the less popular sports for which the competition is less intense. Unless they have a natural talent and truly excel at baseball, basketball or football, it is unlikely that these extremely popular sports will give them an edge in the college admission process. According to ScholarshipStats.com, the percent of high school athletes who go on to compete in college have the best odds for men's fencing (30%), gymnastics (19%), lacrosse (13%), and ice hockey (12%). For women, the best numbers appeared for fencing (38%), ice hockey (24%), lacrosse (13%), and synchronized swimming (12%). Overall, statistics indicate that only 7% of high school athletes go on to play a sport in college.

A similar strategy can be applied to music, as high school orchestras and marching bands attract large numbers of students. Here, too, a little advanced planning can make a big difference. An often repeated-phrase is one uttered by a conductor who referred to the middle section of his orchestra as "Scholarship Row." This is the area that seated students playing oboes, bassoons, bass clarinets, baritone saxophones and tubas.

Students with a bent for dancing might want to develop their skills in a specialized area such as Indian Dance, Hip Hop, Jazz, or Irish Step Dancing. While having fun advancing their talent, they may end up being sought after for the Indian Dance team at Rutgers, the Hip Hop Team at Temple, Ohio State or the University of Delaware, the Jazz Team at Hofstra or the University of Michigan, or the Irish Dance Team at Villanova, Fordham, Georgetown or Boston College.

Students who spend years in Boy Scouts or Girl Scouts can likewise use this worthwhile activity as a launching pad for college. But while it's very impressive for a young man to earn the highest Eagle Scout Award, or a young woman to earn her Gold Award, in reality there are tens of thousands of students who reach the top tier in scouting each year. To make their achievement truly noteworthy to colleges, students should select their culminating project carefully to insure that it demonstrates true leadership qualities and has a long-term, positive impact on its intended community.

Some students pursue more individualized activities. A Florida high school senior gained attention for being offered more than a million dollars in scholarship money. Yes, she was a great student. But the quality that differentiated her from most of her peers was that she had been an equestrian rider since the first grade. After breaking her femur in freshman year, she had picked up "dressage." This is when a rider and horse perform a series of precise, memorized movements. She had earned second place in a national competition.

Close to a thousand students each year are not only accepted to, but also awarded free tuition and housing at, 19 prestigious universities due to their work as golf caddies. Other students, talented in cartooning or video game innovation, are accepted to colleges and awarded scholarship money each year by the National Cartoonist Society Foundation and the Game Show Network.

By choosing an activity that is both fun and purposeful, students can enjoy their afterschool hours while putting themselves on the right track to ultimately impress college admissions officers. The key is for students to stand out from the pack, in whatever activity they choose, and make sure college admission people are aware of their talent.

Stretching Academically

Colleges are most attracted to students who demonstrate intellectual curiosity. Seeking out, and becoming engaged in, academically enriching activities outside of the classroom serves many benefits for high school students. First of all, it helps them stand out from their peers, most of whom are taking the standard course load dictated by the State of New Jersey. Secondly, it helps students identify potential college "majors" by becoming familiar with material in the field. For example, many high school students consider psychology for their college studies because they like helping solve their friends' problems. A college-level course in psychology, the study of the brain, is often eye opening. Likewise, many high school students think about becoming physical therapists. Who wouldn't want a career working out athletes on the Giants, Jets, Eagles, Nets or Yankees rosters? Often a course in human anatomy and physiology puts this potential major into perspective. Expanding the mind by seeking knowledge in any area of interest help students become proficient and adept learners.

Students seeking academic enrichment have a vast array of options. Many high school students take courses at local community colleges where they are most welcome and often offered a discounted tuition. Other students take courses online, where the opportunities are almost limitless. High school students in New Jersey can actually sit at home on their computers and take courses such as *Medical Neuroscience* from Duke University, *Introduction to Computer Science & Programming* from M.I.T., *Understanding Research Methods* from The University of London, *or Particle Physics* from The University of Geneva.

These are just a sample of the thousands of college courses that are offered through online services from many of the most prestigious colleges and universities in the U.S. and 28 other countries. Students are typically able to explore lectures and non-graded material at no cost. However, there is often a charge if students submit assignments to be graded or if students want to receive a certificate upon completion of a course. Five years ago, *edX.org* was founded by Harvard University and M.I.T. as an online learning destination to offer high-quality courses from the world's top universities. It brags that it now offers more than 1,300 courses and has students from every country in the world.

A similar online learning destination is *coursera.org* which offers more than 2,100 courses. Among the most popular topics are: Computer Science, Business, Data Science, Physical Science & Engineering, Social Science, and Arts & Humanities. Both of these online sites host courses in several languages, including English, Spanish, French and Chinese, and offer Introductory, Intermediate, and Advanced level courses. These courses can be extremely beneficial to high school students who are trying to identify a potential college major. By taking an online course in a field of possible interest, students can assess whether or not they enjoy the particular course of study and whether or not they seem to have a natural talent to succeed. Immersing themselves in these courses, whether taking *Game Theory* from Stanford University, *Algorithms* from Princeton University, or *Quantitative Methods* from the University of Amsterdam, is a sure way for college-bound students to add an impressive element to their college applications. Colleges and universities greatly value the quality of intellectual curiosity and will take special note of students who took courses, outside of the required high school curriculum, on their own personal time. What college admissions officer wouldn't be impressed with an essay written by a student who studied *The Quantum World* or *Entrepreneurship in Emerging Economies* with a Harvard University professor?

Getting The Facts

Moving onto college is a huge step for any student. For most, it is the first time they are actually choosing their own school, the city in which they will live, the academic, social and cultural climate with which they will be surrounded, and the future life work for which they will prepare. Students, and their parents, should recognize the enormity of this next chapter in their lives and gather as much information as possible.

It's never too early for students to start considering all of the options that lie ahead. In fact, if they'd like to tour all eight Ivy League schools during one afternoon, while lounging in their bedroom sipping hot chocolate, that's certainly an option. Sites such as "youvisit.com" provide 360-degree virtual tours of more than a thousand colleges worldwide.

If you choose to start at Princeton University, for example, you can experience a virtual tour as a student guide leads you around the campus and shares the academic, cultural and social experiences enjoyed by the Princeton Tigers. If you are interested in a specific location on campus, a click on your keyboard can bring you directly to the Firestone Library, Eating Clubs, Athletic Complex, or Woodrow Wilson School of Public and International Affairs.

Recently, Duke University joined the ranks of schools featured on youvisit.com. A tour of this campus, ranked one of the most beautiful in the country, includes the iconic Duke Chapel and its 210 foot tower that soars above the West Campus. Also featured is the famed Michael W. Krzyzewski (Athletic) Center. Not only are these college tours offered in English, but youvisit.com also offers virtual campus tours in Arabic, Portuguese, Chinese, Hindi and Spanish.

Another popular site, ecampustours.com, offers virtual tours of 1,300 colleges including 11 in New Jersey: Bloomfield College, Montclair State University, Rutgers University at Camden and Newark, Stevens Institute of Technology, Drew University, Princeton University, The College of New Jersey, Felician University, Rowan University and St. Peter's College. This site also offers a gamut of advice for parents and students, including referrals to sites where they can buy, rent and sell textbooks, shop for college apparel, and locate popular dorm items.

A similar site, CampusTours.com, reports that it has been visited by more than seven million students for its virtual tours and maps of 1,700 colleges and universities. The site also features data on everything from admissions statistics to college majors to tuition and room/board costs.

High school students who are experienced at virtual games, virtual shopping, and virtual tutoring, can now add "virtual college touring" to their list of virtual activities.

Using Vacation Time Wisely

While everyone needs a summer break, it's important for students to use their vacation time wisely. Colleges often ask, as one of their essay questions, for students to describe what they did during a recent summer. Impressive essays include stories about volunteer work, internships, and other opportunities where students helped others and/or learned more about themselves.

One great use of the upcoming summer is to take a college course or two. Hundreds of colleges, near and far, will be welcoming high school students for a pre-college experience this summer.

Students seeking the Harvard experience can choose from a wide array of summer courses while living in Harvard Square during a two-week program. The roster of academic courses includes Artificial Intelligence, Digital Media, Regenerative Medicine, Engineering Science, Introduction to College Writing, and Speaking with Power, Passion, and Purpose.

Students favoring the allure of a Washington D.C. summer experience have many opportunities at Georgetown University which is offering the choice of one, three, or five-week programs. Course options include: American Politics, Journalism, Law, Forensic Science, Entrepreneurship, Medical Immersion, Coding & Data Science, and National Security & Counterintelligence.

Closer to home, the "Rutgers Summer Scholars Program" provides high achieving teenagers the opportunity to get a jump start on their college degree, or simply explore an area of interest. This program is open to students aged 16 and above with a minimum GPA of 3.0 (Younger students are considered on a case-by-case basis.) Students can choose from an impressive array of more than 2,000 courses in areas including American Sign Language, Biochemistry, Broadcast Television Production, Digital Game Creation, Entrepreneurship, Macro or Micro Economics, Nature of Politics, and Psychology.

For students interested in exploring engineering as a possible career, Rutgers also hosts a "Pre-Engineering Summer Academy" for rising high school juniors and seniors introducing them to aerospace, biomedical, civil, computer, electrical, forensic, and mechanical engineering. Similarly, students interested in a potential career in Engineering or Medicine may opt for the two-week "Exploring Career Options in Engineering and Science" (ECOES) program at the Stevens Institute of Technology. Other opportunities at this Hoboken-based university include one-week programs in Pre-Med Science and Pre-Med Engineering. In addition to participating in riveting lectures and labs, all of these programs include site visits to Fortune 500 companies.

Thinking of becoming a vet? The "Veterinary Exploration Through Science" (VETS) program at the University of Pennsylvania (UPENN) offers a choice of one-week sessions where students experience veterinary medicine at the university's small animal hospital and participate in labs in pathology, microbiology and anatomy. A longer, two-week course in veterinarian science is offered at Georgetown University, while a three-week program is available at Cornell University.

Contemplating a career in business? The prestigious Wharton School of Business at UPENN hosts the four-week "Wharton Sports Business Academy." Students attend lectures, meet with respected leaders in the sports industry, visit historic sports venues, and create business plans for new sports-focused businesses. Other impressive business-oriented summer programs of varying lengths are offered at a host of universities including Georgetown, Cornell, UCLA and the University of Chicago.

The summer is also a perfect time for students to explore their creative talents. Students planning to major in the visual arts may want to spend the summer developing their portfolio. There are National Portfolio Days through the country each fall, including one in Philadelphia and one in Manhattan each November, where college representatives critique the work of high school students. Students who prepare in advance can maximize this opportunity to present their work to an array of potential colleges.

Students with a love of writing can use the summer to write and publish a book on any topic, at little-to-no cost, with the help of Amazon's "CreateSpace" site. Joining the world of published authors is a sure way to impress college admissions officers.

Regardless of their area of interest, students should make sure they will have a compelling story to tell if asked, "What did you do during your most recent summer?"

Part II. It's All About "The Test"

Why and When Students Should Take PSAT

Hundreds of thousands of high school students throughout the country take the PSAT exam each October, but many don't understand its significance. Students and parents often believe the "P" in PSAT stands for practice and that the test is merely a trial run for the all-important SAT exam. In reality, the "P" does not stand for practice, or anything else, and it is so much more than a student's first attempt at a college entrance exam.

Another name for the PSAT is the NMSQT, which *does* stand for something – National Merit Scholarship Qualifying Test. High school *juniors* who take the PSAT/NMSQT are on the official route of entry to the National Merit Scholarship Program. Fifty thousand high scoring students each year ultimately qualify for program recognition, which carries considerable prestige. Of these students, two-thirds end up receiving Letters of Commendation, but are not awarded scholarship money. One-third of these students ultimately qualify as Semi-finalists and move on to compete for National Merit Scholarships which are awarded to 7,500 students annually.

The vast majority of high school juniors take the PSAT/NMSQT, not only to be eligible for recognition and/or scholarship money, but also to get on the radar of colleges nationwide. The College Board, which produces the PSAT (and SAT exams) shares information provided by students, such as their current GPA and potential college major, with colleges and universities. These schools often send informational material, and sometimes college application fee waivers, to students whom they identify to be potential applicants. It's encouraging for students to receive unsolicited information from colleges that seem eager to attract them.

High school sophomores, and even freshmen, often choose to take the PSAT exam. But the exam is strictly a trial run for them as their scores are not eligible for National Merit consideration. Since the PSAT is simply a shorter version of the SAT exam, with the same level of difficulty, covering the exact same academic material, students find it extremely helpful to do SAT preparation prior to their PSAT as it then benefits them for both exams.

Facts of the SAT

The advice of *U.S. News & World Report*, whose guidebook (*Best Colleges*) is basically the bible to the college industry, is for students to start taking the SAT exam early in their high school years for several reasons.

First of all, students can now take the SAT as many times as they want and (most) colleges will never know how many times they take the test. When the time comes for students to submit their scores to colleges, they can choose their highest scores, even "super-scoring" (mixing and matching), to send their best Math score from one test and their best Reading/Writing score from another test.

Another advantage to students who start taking the SAT early is that their first test can serve as a baseline, indicating what areas they need to hone. Then, as students practice for subsequent tests, either on their own or with the help of a private tutor or prep course, they can get measurable results and track their improvement. It's also a good idea to get that first SAT experience, which is likely to be stress-ridden, out of the way so students can be a bit more relaxed on future sittings.

Students can also use early SAT scores to influence their choice of high school courses. Those struggling in Math would want to get through Algebra I and II early in their high school years, as one third of SAT Math questions are in the category "Heart of Algebra." If weaknesses in reading comprehension or grammar are resulting in low scores on the Evidence-Based Reading and Writing sections, students can likewise choose classes to strengthen these literary skills.

Even students who may not be bound for a four-year college should prepare for, and take, the SAT exam. Although community "junior" colleges typically do not require SAT scores for admission, these test scores are required to be eligible for many college scholarships. Respectable SAT scores also exempt community college applicants from taking placement exams that may result in placement in "remedial" (non-credit) courses. In addition, if a student seeks to transfer from a community college to a four-year college without first completing a certain number of credits, the college the student is applying to will usually want to review SAT scores. And, even after graduating from college, students are often asked by potential employers to produce SAT scores. According to The Wall Street Journal, consulting firms, software companies and investment banks are among the most common employers who ask job candidates to dig up their SAT scores.

Taking the SAT early can give all students, regardless of their academic strengths or weaknesses, the time and motivation needed to improve their scores. Students can continue taking the SAT as many times as they want throughout their high school years. The test is offered each year in October, November, December, March, May, June and August. College Board keeps a record of each student's scores. When the time comes to apply to their colleges of choice, students simply log into their College Board account and pick and choose the scores they want to send. (While the vast majority of colleges allow students to send their highest scores, there are some colleges that require all scores to be reported.) By preparing diligently for this all-important test, and taking it as many times as necessary to reach their potential, students can greatly increase their chances of getting accepted into their college of choice – hopefully with scholarship money to help foot the bill.

How To Maximize SAT Scores

Students should be thoroughly familiar with the format and content of the SAT exam well in advance of their test date. It is *not a secret* what the test looks like or what material will be covered on each test section. (For example, there is always one trigonometry question and the only rule students need to know to answer it correctly is that, in a right triangle, Sine X = Cos Y.)

It's vital for students to know, and understand, the directions for each test section in advance so they can use all of the allotted time to earn points rather than to figure out what they need to do. This is particularly important for the open-ended math questions where students have to solve questions that are *not* multiple-choice and then correctly bubble in their answers. Students need to know, for example, that if their answer is *one and a half* and they bubble in the four boxes to read 11/2 they will not get credit, as the computer will record it as eleven halves. (Correct answers are 1.5 or 3/2)

It's important for students to understand how this test is scored. For all test questions, students earn one point for each correct answer. There is no longer a ¼ point deduction for incorrect answers, so students should guess when in doubt. Since the multiple-choice questions have four options (A, B C and D), even random guessing will provide correct answers approximately 25% of the time!

Students should first focus on the easier questions, since an easy question counts just as much as a hard question. College Board does not want students to get a perfect score, so there are some questions on each section intended to frustrate students. When students face such a question, they should cross out any answer choices they do not like, take a good guess from the remaining choices, and move on.

While these are a few of the general SAT test-taking tips, all of the strategies and secrets of acing the SAT are available in the SAT Smart Strategy Guide at the beginning of this book. It is also available online at www.SATsmart.com.

Once students are well versed on the strategies of the test, the most effective way to prepare is by using official test material by College Board, the company that produces the SAT. *The Official SAT Study Guide* contains eight full-length practice exams, including a few actual exams that were offered over the past few years. Here, students can gain expertise on material that will mirror exactly what they will face on the day of their test. They can become proficient on the four sections of the test, as well as the optional essay.

The first section of the SAT is Critical Reading. Students are presented with five passages (one of which is a double story), each followed by ten or eleven questions. Students need to be particularly careful when answering the "duo" questions. That's when they're asked to draw a conclusion from the passage and then, in a follow-up question, to identify the specific textual evidence in the passage. Students should also be mindful of the "vocabulary in context" questions whereby they are given a specific line in the passage to refer back to and asked to choose the best replacement for the vocabulary word. Students earn between 100 to 400 points for this section.

The second section of the SAT is Writing and Language. This section is comprised of four "stories," each followed by eleven questions focused on errors in sentence structure, tense, word choice, punctuation, and clarity of writing. Students earn between 100 and 400 points on this section as well. A student's scores for these two sections, Critical Reading and Writing and Language, are added together providing an "Evidence-based Reading and Writing" score in the range of 200 to 800 points.

The third section of the SAT is Math *without* a calculator, while the fourth section is Math *with* a calculator. Both sections present a table of formulas at the top of the section, reminding students of geometric formulas they may need to use. Each of the two Math sections begins with multiple-choice questions, which increase in difficulty from easy to hard. Each Math section concludes with open-ended questions, which likewise increase in difficulty. Students should be sure they thoroughly understand, going into the test, exactly how to bubble in the open-ended answers in order to get credit for their work. Students should use their test booklet as scrap paper, as none will be provided. The test booklet is not sacred, and can be written all over. Students should solve problems on their test paper, making each problem as visual as possible by drawing diagrams, labeling sides and angles of triangles, etc. There are 20 questions on Section 3, and 38 questions on Section 4, of the SAT. Students earn a score in the range of 200 to 800 points based on the number of questions they answer correctly out of the combined 58 questions.

The last section of the SAT exam is the optional essay. While students are not required to register for and complete this section, it is advisable that they do so as the essay is required by many colleges. The essay section requires students to read a passage that typically ranges from 650 to 750 words, and then write an essay explaining how the author builds a persuasive argument. Students are provided with four lined pages on which to write their essay, and a time frame of 50 minutes. Since it comes at the end of a three-hour exam, it's no surprise that many students would rather opt out of this section. But it's important for students to realize that although College Board considers the section optional, many colleges – particularly the more competitive ones – require that the essay be completed in order to consider a student's SAT scores.

Most students, at the time they take the SAT, do not have a finalized list of the colleges to which they will ultimately apply. Even when students think they know where they will be sending their applications, they often learn of other suitable choices and expand their college list. So it's never a good idea for students to limit their options.

Most New Jersey students apply to one or more in-state colleges, where they can benefit from the lower cost of in-state tuition. If Rutgers University - New Brunswick, The College of New Jersey, or Rowan University are of interest, students should be sure to complete the essay as it is required, or "recommended," by all of these institutions. It is likewise required by Princeton University, but not by Monmouth, Montclair State, Rider or Seton Hall universities. So for most students, it makes good sense to write the essay at the conclusion of the exam and know that they have covered all the bases!

Power of Impressive SAT Scores

Jeff Bezos, the billionaire founder and CEO of Amazon, is one of the most famous advocates of using SAT scores in the hiring process. "Hiring only the best and brightest was key to Amazon's success," claimed Bezos, who himself scored highly on standardized tests from the time he was a young child. Amazon is not the only big name company to request SAT scores of its job applicants. According to The Wall Street Journal, impressive consulting firms such as McKinsey and Bain, and leading banks including Goldman Sachs, are among the companies that ask about SAT scores on their job applications. And this is not the case just for recent college grads seeking their first full-time jobs. Mid-life workers who have garnered real world life and work experience, for whom their high school SAT experience is a decades old memory, are often asked to report their scores.

The reason SAT scores may stick with people throughout their lives is that it's both standardized and objective. Everyone takes the SAT at approximately the same time in life at roughly the same level of education (16-18 year olds in junior or senior year of high school). The test is marked on a curve, so an individual's SAT score represents how well he or she scored in comparison to peers. Jonathan Wai, an intelligence expert and researcher at Duke University's *Talent Identification Program*, says the SATs are considered to be a measure of "general intelligence and general ability." He added that research has shown that general ability "actually predicts occupational success across a range of occupations."

Unless hiring policies change, millions of students currently in college already know that a future career with Amazon Corporate is probably not in the cards!

What About the ACT?

High school students planning to attend college know that a standardized college admission exam lies in their future. For almost a century, the test of choice was the SAT. It was created in 1926 to allow college-bound students to take one entrance exam for several universities instead of taking a separate entrance exam for each university to which they applied. Its purpose, also, was to provide equal opportunity for all students to demonstrate their skills and knowledge regardless of their economic status and their specific high school curriculum. Approximately 8,000 students took the first SAT in 1926; ninety years later, that number climbed to 1.7 million students.

But the SAT does have competition. The ACT, which was created in 1959 for basically the same purposes as the SAT, is most popular with students in mid-America, while students on both the east and west coasts of the U.S., and in Texas, favor the SAT. Statistics from The Washington Post cite that New Jersey students greatly prefer the SAT with more than 84,000 sitting for the SAT compared to 24,000 for the ACT in a recent year. Almost every college in the U.S. will accept either SAT or ACT scores (and no college requires both). So what's the difference?

With the redesign of the SAT in 2016, both tests are now remarkably similar in that they both have one Critical Reading section and one English section (where students identify grammatical errors). They also both offer students an optional essay. The main difference is that the SAT contains two Math sections, whereas the ACT requires students to do one Math section and one Science section (filled with tables, charts and graphs). Also, the SAT provides a box of formulas at the beginning of each Math section, while the ACT does not.

While both tests have roughly the same time frame, with the new SAT at 3 hours and the ACT five minutes shorter (without the optional essay), there are considerably more questions on the ACT requiring students to work at a substantially quicker pace. The complete SAT contains 154 questions while the ACT is comprised of 215 questions -- 40% more questions than the SAT.

The scoring scale for the SAT and ACT varies greatly. The ACT is scored on a scale ranging from 0 to 36 for each area of the test while the SAT is scored on a scale ranging from 200 to 800. The median SAT score of roughly 1000 converts to an ACT score of 21.

Since both of these tests are marked on a curve, students are basically competing with their peers when taking either test. So the key is preparation. Standardized test scores are the main criteria that colleges use when allocating scholarship money, as it's the fairest way to compare students from a wide range of backgrounds and educational experiences. By improving their SAT (or ACT) scores, students can significantly increase their chances of being awarded scholarship money – and whatever money they are awarded for freshman year typically gets renewed for each of the student's subsequent three years of college. For example, an extra $8,000 merit award – due to higher SAT or ACT scores – ultimately becomes $32,000 of scholarship money.

So the best strategy for college-bound students is to choose one exam to take – either the SAT or ACT – and devote some serious time and effort to preparation. The payoff could be substantial.

What About Test Optional Colleges?

There are hundreds of colleges (including community "junior" colleges) that do not require SAT or ACT scores as part of their application process. Many students find this extremely attractive and are thrilled at the prospect of avoiding a lengthy test preparation and test-taking process. But students should be sure to check the fine print for each college they are considering, as eliminating standardized tests from the college admission process could have serious repercussions. Many colleges and universities that say they are "test optional" actually require test scores for out-of-state applicants. Others require test scores for students seeking enrollment in certain programs, particularly in the field of science. Students with low grade point averages (GPA) are often required to submit SAT or ACT scores to test optional colleges.

Some colleges that do not require SAT or ACT scores require other standardized tests, which many students consider to be even more difficult, such as SAT II Subject Tests, Advanced Placement (AP) exams, or International Baccalaureate exams. Another reason students shouldn't be too quick to skip the SAT and/or ACT is that many test optional colleges only award merit scholarship money to students who have submitted test scores. So students who get accepted to these colleges may find that, in the end, they are not able to afford to attend.

For students who are still convinced that test optional is the way to go, there are many colleges to choose from within New Jersey and neighboring states. Some of the more popular test optional universities in New Jersey include: Drew, Montclair State and Rowan. New York hosts Hofstra University, Marist, Wagner and Ithaca colleges, Long Island University, New School, Julliard School, and Fashion Institute of Technology.

Test optional schools in Connecticut include: Fairfield, Sacred Heart and Quinnipiac universities and Mitchell and Trinity colleges. Heading south, other test optional schools include the University of Delaware, Maryland's Loyola University, and, in Washington DC, American and George Washington universities and The Catholic University of America. Since the roster of test optional colleges changes each year, it's important to view the current list at www.fairtest.org

Don't Forget About AP and SAT II Exams

The highest level of courses offered in high school is Advanced Placement (AP) courses. They are offered in a wide variety of more than 30 academic subjects, including Studio Arts, Music Theory, Psychology, Micro and Macro Economics, Government and Politics, Calculus, Statistics, Biology, Chemistry, Physics, U.S. and World History, and many foreign languages including Chinese, Japanese, Spanish, French, German and Italian. Not every high school offers the full gamut of AP courses, and some high schools do not offer any at all.

The good news about AP courses is that they give students an opportunity to do college level work while still in high school. Towards the end of the school year, in early May, students can take AP exams which are written by College Board – the same company that offers the PSAT and SAT. AP exams are typically about three hours long, and students are graded on a scale of 1 to 5. Students who score a 5 or 4 on an AP exam are frequently offered college credits. Some colleges even offer credit for an AP score of 3.

The bad news about AP courses is that they can add additional stress to a student's high school experience. When high school students apply to competitive colleges, the criteria for acceptance includes consideration of how competitive a course load the students took. When a high school offers a vast number of AP courses, top students often feel obliged to take as many of these courses as possible in order to be competitive with their peers with whom they may be vying for the same college seats.

Ideally, students who are academically prepared to do college level work should choose AP courses in subjects compatible to their college plans. In other words, students planning to enter the medical field might take AP Biology and/or Chemistry. Students with hopes of becoming engineers or architects might favor AP Calculus. Students who are considering a college major in Psychology or Economics would do well to take the coinciding AP course in high school to confirm their talent for, and interest in, the field.

Students who take several AP courses during their high school years, and are successful on their AP exams, should take note of which colleges offer credit for the courses. Most colleges do offer credit; but some do not. By attending a college that gives credit for high scoring AP exams, students have greater opportunities to take additional courses. This often allows students to double major, take a major and a minor, or even graduate a semester or year early.

High school students eyeing the most competitive colleges also need to keep SAT II exams, known as Subject Tests, in mind. In order to apply to many of the most elite colleges and universities, students not only have to report impressive scores on the SAT (originally referred to as the SAT I Reasoning Test) but also on two SAT II exams. These exams are offered in a wide variety of subjects: Math (Levels 1 & 2), Biology, Chemistry, Physics, Literature, U.S. History, World History, Spanish, French, Chinese, Italian, German, Modern Hebrew, Latin, Japanese, and Korean. They are all one hour in length and are graded on a scale of 200-800. (Students who choose to submit ACT scores are not required to take SAT II exams.)

Students should take SAT II exams at the end of the school year in which they are taking the specific subject. For example, if studying Honors or AP Biology as a sophomore, students should take the SAT II Biology exam in either May or June of that academic year when they will have the greatest chance of success. According to the College Board website, there are more than 400 colleges and universities that require, recommend, or consider SAT Subject Tests in the admissions process.

Part III. Finding The Ideal College

New Jersey's "Brain Drain"

New Jersey is known for its "brain drain" – with about 30,000 high school graduates heading out of state for college each year, leaving behind about 25,000 to attend in-state colleges and universities, according to Federal data. These statistics make New Jersey one of the top exporters of students. While more than half of all college-bound students leave our state – they don't go far!

Where do migrating students go? The Chronicle of Higher Education tracked the entering college freshmen class of 2014-15 and found that the vast majority of students are attracted to schools in nearby states. University of Delaware was the most popular, enrolling 895 NJ students. Penn State came in second, enrolling 884 NJ students, and Drexel (in Philadelphia) came in third, enrolling 631 students from the Garden State. NYU was the fourth most popular, enrolling some 600 NJ students, followed by three Philadelphia area universities: Villanova, Temple, and St. Joseph's.

The top ten were rounded out with Syracuse (NY), Lehigh (PA) and the University of Maryland at College Park. It's not that New Jersey is lacking colleges. It houses 19 public community colleges where many high school graduates choose to begin their education and strive to earn an associate degree without accumulating substantial student debt. New Jersey is also home to 11 public four-year colleges and universities, with highly regarded Rutgers University enrolling about 65,000 students spread over campuses in New Brunswick, Piscataway, Newark and Camden. Also, New Jersey boasts 15 private colleges and universities, including Princeton University, which is often ranked as the premiere college in the country, and Seton Hall University and Fairleigh Dickinson University, which are the state's largest.

Why does this brain drain exist? New Jersey is a small state, making it easy for students to cross the border to attend college while still remaining close to home. New Jersey is also an expensive state. The high cost of attending college in New Jersey -- even the public universities -- makes out-of-state schools extremely attractive when they offer substantial grant, or scholarship funds.

Colleges in neighboring states actively recruit New Jersey students because they view New Jersey as having many stellar high schools and strong applicants. Colleges and universities that round out the list of "Top 25 schools with the most NJ students" are: Towson (MD), University of Rhode Island, University of Scranton (PA), James Madison (VA), Boston University (MA), University of Pittsburgh (PA), University of Michigan, Cornell University (NY), George Washington University (Washington D.C.), Pace University (NY), Johnson & Wales University (RI), Quinnipiac University (CT), West Chester University (PA), Northeastern University (MA), and Loyola University (MD).

Benefits of Attending College In-State

One of the main advantages for New Jersey students to attend college in-state is a financial benefit. Students who rank in the top 15 percent of their high school class, at the end of either junior or senior year, may be eligible for the NJ Stars program. This covers the cost of tuition at all of New Jersey's 19 community colleges for up to five semesters, as long as students maintain a grade point average of 3.0 or higher. This program offers students the opportunity to earn their Associates degree without taking on college debt.

The NJ Stars II program is a continuation of the NJ Stars program. It provides students who successfully earned their Associate's degree with a 3.25 grade point average or higher with funding to transfer to a New Jersey four year college or university to seek a bachelor's degree. NJ Stars II students are eligible for up to $2,500 annually.

Even students who do not participate in the New Jersey Stars program benefit financially by being entitled to pay the discounted "in-state" tuition and fees rate at any of New Jersey's 11 public four-year colleges and universities. The discount is substantial! For example, annual out-of-state tuition and fees at Rutgers University - New Brunswick is currently $30,579 as opposed to in-state tuition and fees of $14,638. Similarly, annual out-of-state tuition and fees at The College of New Jersey is currently $27,577 as opposed to in-state tuition and fees of $16,148.

Students who flee New Jersey to attend University of Delaware are billed at the annual out-of-state tuition and fees rate of $33,150 rather than the in-state rate of $13,160. The same is true at the very popular Penn State-University Park where annual out-of-state tuition and fees is $33,664 compared to the in-state rate of $18,436. It often makes sense from a financial point of view for NJ students to seek the benefits of higher education right here in the Garden State.

Research is Key

While it's extremely valuable to know which colleges are popular with New Jersey students, both in and out of state, it's vital for all families to do their own research. A college investment is one of the largest expenses that most families will face in their lifetime. So the key is to do some serious homework to identify best-fit colleges where each particular student can prepare for the career of his/her dreams, at an affordable cost, with the likelihood of earning an impressive salary over the course of a career.

A good place for families to start their research is at www.CollegeBoard.org. There they will find a College Search database that contains information on more than 2,000 four-year colleges in the United States. As students select the specific criteria that are important to them, such as school size, location, availability of on-campus housing, choice of major, etc., the list of appropriate colleges starts to shrink. For example, if a student clicks on "location" and chooses New Jersey, Delaware and Pennsylvania as options, the list shrinks to 176 potential colleges. If the student then clicks "campus housing" and indicates that he/she wants on-campus housing available for all four years, the list further reduces to 57 good-fit colleges. If the student then identifies psychology as the major of choice, the list identifies 48 potential colleges. Without leaving their computer, students can vastly narrow down the list of colleges worthy of further investigation!

Once a manageable list of appropriate colleges has been developed, students should carefully examine the website of each of these colleges. Then, for more objective information, look into the latest issue of U.S. News & World Report's *America's Best Colleges.* This annual magazine ranks colleges and offers a great deal of helpful information about each college in the U.S. including acceptance rate, average SAT scores, diversity of students, average size of classes, most popular majors, and retention rate (the percentage of students who return for their sophomore year). Retention rate is an excellent indicator of how happy students are with the quality of any particular college or university.

Comparing statistics can be extremely helpful, even among colleges right here in the Garden State. New Jersey boasts 28 four-year institutions of higher education, each with its own strengths and attractions. The College of New Jersey (TCNJ), ranked as the #1 public regional university in the north, boasts a 94% freshmen retention rate and 47% of its classes have fewer than 20 students. Rutgers University – New Brunswick and Stevens Institute of Technology tied as #69 in the category of best national universities. Their freshmen retention rates are 92% and 94%, respectively. Rutgers offers a selection of more than 150 majors and minors, making it attractive to students who have not yet chosen a career path. Stevens Institute is highly regarded for its stellar education in fields of engineering, with its most popular majors including mechanical, civil, electrical, and chemical engineering. Since students are also concerned about their likelihood of securing gainful employment in their field of study after graduation, *U.S. News & World Reports* now includes postgraduate salary information on 1,000 schools.

Of course, a key criterion in choosing a college should be to get the best value possible for your tuition dollars. *Money* magazine also releases annual rankings. It takes into consideration educational quality, affordability, and alumni earnings. *Money* includes a "value added" grade based on how well students typically perform at particular colleges vs. what would be expected based on their economic and academic backgrounds. *Money* screens out any colleges with graduation rates below the median as well as those facing financial difficulties.

Of course, students typically worry about their chances of getting accepted to an impressive college or university. A little research, here too, can help put into perspective the likelihood of meeting with success. *Money* publishes a list of *The 50 Best Colleges You Can Actually Get Into*, and it includes many favorites of New Jersey students. The schools listed, which all accept more than 50% of their applicants, include many that are popular with New Jersey students: Rutgers University – New Brunswick, Muhlenberg College, James Madison University, Texas A & M, Virginia Tech, University of Delaware, Manhattan College, Clemson University, and Massachusetts Maritime Academy.

Once students and parents are armed with all of the factual information they can find about their colleges of interest, it's time to attend college fairs. These take place at many high schools throughout New Jersey and admission is always free. Typically, representatives from over 100 colleges, universities, technical schools, and the military host tables filled with materials, and are happy to answer individual questions. These local fairs provide the perfect opportunity for "one stop shopping" to gather materials and answers to all college-related questions.

There are also national college fairs, including one typically held in April at the Meadowlands in Secaucus. The grand scope of this event provides the opportunity for students to attend workshops on topics including: College Search Process, How to Write a Great College Essay, College Athletics, Performing Arts, Applying to Health Professions, Test Optional Admissions, and Financial Aid and Scholarships.

To make the most of these opportunities, students should do their homework in advance. They should make a list of the colleges in which they are specifically interested, and the questions to which they are seeking answers. Then, while talking to each college representative, students should ask for a business card. Once home, students should email the reps of colleges in which they are particularly interested, thanking them for their time and information and expressing interest in their school. This is the basis of establishing a relationship with the college rep who is often the very same person who will be making the decision as to whom is accepted or rejected from the school.

Touring Colleges

There is nothing like touring the grounds of a college campus and experiencing, first hand, what the school has to offer. But with more than 3,500 two and four-year colleges in the U.S., and more than 800 colleges within 300 miles of central New Jersey, students should narrow down their search to potential "good fit colleges" before embarking on their road trips.

Visiting a college when classes are in session allows high school students to take in the atmosphere and to visualize what it would be like to be a part of the student body. New Jersey students should utilize the days they are off from school, which are not college holidays, to schedule these tours. Columbus Day, Election Day, the November Teacher Convention days (in many New Jersey school districts) and Presidents' Day often provide perfect opportunities to investigate, first-hand, colleges of interest.

Spring break is typically another perfect opportunity for high school students to tour college campuses while classes, activities, and college life are in full swing. Colleges tend to schedule their spring breaks in early March, while high schools hold them in late March or April. So it's an ideal time for high school students to visit colleges and start to identify which schools may, or may not, be potential "good fit" colleges.

If parents are available during a student's spring break, it's a perfect time for a road trip to visit out-of-town colleges. The vast majority of students attend college within five hours of home, so the destination does *not* need to be a far off locale. If a student dreams of attending a big city school, then a tour of colleges in the Boston or Washington D.C. areas may prove fruitful. If a student prefers a suburban or rural environment, then a drive through Pennsylvania offers an option of touring close to 100 different colleges and universities.

Students who are on their own during spring break can still put the week to great use. By visiting two of New Jersey's highly-ranked schools, The College of New Jersey (TCNJ) and Rutgers University, students can quickly come to the realization of the type of college they prefer.

TCNJ hosts about 6,500 students on a tranquil, suburban campus. The school's most popular majors are Teacher Education, Business, and Biological Sciences, and almost all classes have 25 or fewer students.

Rutgers University in New Brunswick is home to more than 35,000 students in a distinctly urban setting. The list of majors is almost limitless, and class size can exceed 300 students.

Students visiting both of these colleges/universities seldom like them equally. They usually find themselves drawn to one atmosphere over the other, and can use this self-awareness in choosing other colleges to visit in the future. For example, students who like TCNJ often find Villanova and Lehigh to be appealing. Those who prefer Rutgers often look favorably upon Penn State and New York University (NYU).

The most important aspect of a college visit is the official tour. It's important for students to contact colleges ahead of time to schedule their campus tours which are usually offered every weekday, both in the morning and the afternoon. Students should register in advance for a specific tour, and then be sure to sign in when they arrive on the day of their visit. The reason this is vital is that colleges track student interest. When reviewing college applications, admissions officers check to see if the student had actually visited the campus – an indication that the student is a serious applicant. When students live within a few hours of a college, and do not visit prior to filing an application, the admissions team often interprets this as a lack of real interest in the school. College admissions people favor students who they believe will actually attend their school, if offered the chance to do so.

Students should take notes during their college tours. At the time of each tour students think they will remember exactly what they are seeing and being told. But problems arise after students have visited several colleges, and start mixing up the details of the various schools. By writing down the specifics of what is most appealing about each college, students will be well on their way to filing successful applications.

When students later get to work on their college applications, they should personalize each one by emphasizing the qualities that most attract them to each particular college. This is where the notes they took during their tours come in very handy. Was there a particular major that appealed to them? Are there enticing internship opportunities? Is there a study abroad program in an exotic location that would tie in well with a particular course of study? By personalizing each application, students gain an impressive advantage in the competitive college application process. Admissions people strongly favor students who have done their homework and know where they want to spend their college years!

As for the college tours, most originate at the Campus Center, which typically houses the main cafeteria, or food court, as well as the bookstore and a host of amenities. Students with strong dietary preferences or restrictions should pay particular attention to the culinary offerings, as the campus dining facility would provide them with breakfast, lunch and dinner for most of their college meals. Other attractions found here may include cinemas, bowling alleys, billiard, ping-pong and air hockey tables, climbing walls, scores of TVs, coffee bars, convenience stores, banks, beauty salons, meeting rooms and study lounges.

Continuing on to the athletic facilities, most college tours will highlight their stadiums and gymnasiums, but some offer so much more. Top athletic colleges today often feature such amenities as underground practice fields, ice hockey and skating arenas, hydrotherapy pools, saunas, rehabilitation facilities, and theaters for press conferences. Some even boast a golf course or ski slope. For student athletes, such luxuries can serve as a big draw.

Moving on to the more academic-oriented facilities, many colleges feature impressive museums in the fields of art, natural history, anthropology and natural science. Other colleges host state-of-the art engineering laboratories in areas such as biomedical engineering, digital signal processing, and robotics and intelligent systems. There are also colleges that are medically oriented with simulation laboratories that give students hands-on clinical experience. These labs feature rooms occupied by high-tech mannequins that simulate symptoms, diseases and conditions that future doctors are likely to face in hospitals. The "maternity room" at Penn State University even features a mannequin that gives birth (to a baby mannequin).

After students tour a campus, eat in the dining hall, visit the Campus Center, observe all of the amenities, and chat with current students, it usually becomes crystal clear whether or not it's a place they'd like to call home for the next four years.

Choosing a College Major

As millions of students head off to college this fall, well-meaning parents often encourage them to choose the major of their dreams. Sometimes, students have known for years the particular career that would be perfect for them. Other times, students enter college "undecided" and end up making a decision as they move through their coursework. But few students realize the economic impact of their choices.

On average, an individual with a bachelor's degree earns nearly twice the lifetime income of someone with a high school diploma. But just as significant – from a monetary point of view – is the choice of major that can either launch a student into a high paying career or leave the graduate struggling to pay off skyrocketing student debt. In fact, college graduates with the highest-paying majors earn $3.4 million more than those with the lowest-paying majors, over the course of their careers, according to a study by the Georgetown University Center of Education and the Workforce.

The choice of major can have an even bigger impact on future earnings than the choice of school, according to PayScale, an online salary, benefits and compensation information company. So which majors reap the greatest reward for your tuition and time? Hands down, engineering. In fact, the *2016-2017 College Salary Report* by PayScale listed various fields of Engineering in nine of the top ten spots. (Actuarial Science ranked third.)

Petroleum Engineering, which took the top spot with a mid-career annual salary of $172,000, is offered as a major at many campuses of Penn State University and at several Texas universities. Systems Engineering, which came in second, is offered at the University of Pennsylvania (UPenn), the University of Pittsburgh, and Drexel University. Chemical Engineering, which tied with Actuarial Science for third place, is offered at Princeton, Rutgers, and Rowan universities, New Jersey Institute of Technology (NJIT), Stevens Institute of Technology, New York University (NYU), Lehigh University, Lafayette College, and the University of Delaware. Tied for fifth place was Computer Science & Engineering and Nuclear Engineering. The former can be found at The College of New Jersey (TCNJ), Villanova University, Hofstra University, the University of Scranton, and the University of Connecticut. The latter is offered at Massachusetts Institute of Technology (MIT), NYU, and many campuses of Penn State University.

Of course, these are national statistics that do not take into account the various job climates in different parts of the country. In New Jersey, for example, the highest-paying industries are Pharmaceutical Research & Development and Pharmaceutical Manufacturing. The reason is simply that New Jersey is home to some of the world's largest pharmaceutical companies, including Novartis, Johnson & Johnson, Bristol-Myers Squibb, and Merck. Other high paying fields in the Garden State are Information Technology and Financial Services.

Of course, there are always different ways of looking at things. The billionaire investor Mark Cuban, who attained celebrity status for his role on the highly rated ABC-TV show *Shark Tank*, garnered a great deal of attention for views he expressed at the NBA All-Star Technology Summit. (Cuban is the owner of the Dallas Mavericks basketball team.)

Cuban warned that millions of jobs are at risk of becoming automated in the coming years, and feared that even people with in-demand skills, such as computer coding, could soon be displaced. Citing "the automation of automation," Cuban suggested that computers could soon learn how to write software better than humans. His advice to college bound students is to major in the liberal arts. "The nature of jobs is changing," according to Cuban, who recommended English, Philosophy, and foreign languages as some of the majors that will do well in the future job market. Cuban believes that people with "soft skills," such as creative thinking, adaptability, and communication, will have the advantage in an automated workforce.

This advice differs from that offered by the online job-posting site *Indeed*, which listed the best college majors for landing high-paying jobs in growing fields. *Indeed* favored positions that are at low risk for automation, utilize transferable skills, and are in high demand by employers.

Computer and information sciences earned the top spot due to high salaries and skill sets that are transferable across industries. Engineering came in second place, specifically for software, systems, electrical and biomedical engineering. Rounding out the top six recommended fields of study are: Architecture, Business administration/International business, Health professions, and Finance.

College-bound students need to consider both the high-compensation fields of today, and the likely scenario of the job market of the future, when choosing their course of study. They should carefully consider all of the ramifications of their potential major before starting college, as it is always preferable to enter college with a chosen major, rather than "undecided." The reasons for this revolve around both time and money.

Students who enter college "undecided," or who change their major after beginning their studies, frequently end up spending more than four years at their college/university in order to meet the graduation requirements of the major. Also, when students begin their college studies "undecided," they later have to apply to be admitted to the department of their choice. There is no guarantee they will be accepted. So, once students decide that they want to be business majors, for example, if they are not admitted to the College of Business they either have to change their career path or transfer to a different college.

On the other hand, college-bound students who know what they want to do with their life can often cut years of education, a great deal of stress, and a substantial amount of money from their higher education experience.

Many colleges offer dual degree programs whereby students move right into a Masters or Doctorate degree program upon completing their undergraduate education. They do not have to take entrance exams, eliminating the need to repeat the stressful process of preparing for, and taking, standardized tests. Basically, as long as they meet certain requirements during their undergraduate years, they move right into the advanced degree program in their chosen field. These programs are particularly popular in the medical field with combined programs offered for those seeking to become doctors, physician assistants, and physical therapists. While some combined programs, particularly those preparing students to become doctors, take the traditional eight years, others combine the undergraduate and medical school experience into seven years. Several local colleges have combined programs with Drexel University's College of Medicine. Students can start out at Lehigh University, Temple University, or Muhlenberg College for an eight-year experience. Or, they can start out at Drexel University or Villanova University for a seven-year experience.

There are also combined seven and eight year programs between New Jersey Medical School and several New Jersey schools: Caldwell University, Drew University, Montclair State University, New Jersey Institute of Technology, The College of New Jersey, Rutgers University, and Stevens Institute of Technology. This program does require students to take the MCAT and meet other stringent qualifications.

Students seeking to become physician assistants or physical therapists often seek combined six-year programs. Popular colleges/universities in New Jersey and neighboring states offering this opportunity for one or both of these fields include: Seton Hall University, Drexel University, University of Scranton, Quinnipiac University and Ithaca College.

Students with a passion for business might consider a 4 + 1 program, combining their undergraduate degree with a Masters in Business Administration. This eliminates the need to deal with the GMAT exam and cuts one year off the typically two-year M.B.A. experience. Popular schools offering this option include: Fordham University, Penn State University, Fairfield University, Seton Hall University, University of Scranton, Drexel University and Quinnipiac University. Basically, students with a clearly defined career goal, a high G.P.A. and impressive SAT scores, can head off to college knowing they will graduate with the highest degree needed for success in their chosen field.

Even students who are not looking far ahead, trying to tie their bachelors degree to an advanced degree, can benefit greatly by having a sense of direction as they head to college. Not everyone is an A+ student with perfect SAT scores. Students with less than stellar grades and test scores can particularly benefit by knowing the academic field they wish to pursue, as many extremely impressive colleges look for students who are the right match for their programs.

Maritime Academies, for example, have recently earned accolades as their graduates attain among the highest-paying entry-level jobs. Both the Massachusetts Maritime Academy and the California Maritime Academy accept more than 60 percent of their applicants.

STEM (Science, Technology, Engineering and Math) graduates are likewise in high demand for well paying jobs. Fortunately, some very prestigious colleges are more accessible than students imagine. Stonehill College, in Easton, Massachusetts, reports a 94 percent acceptance rate for early decision candidates and offers a great "back door" into the prestigious University of Notre Dame. Students who major in engineering at Stonehill, and maintain a "B" average for three years, are guaranteed admission into Notre Dame for two years and are awarded both a Bachelor of Arts and a Bachelor of Science degree. Another highly-regarded "tech" school, Virginia Tech, has an acceptance rate of over 70% and very competitive annual tuition rates of less than $13,000 for in-state students and less than $30,000 for out-of-state students.

Students seeking a career in nursing would do well to consider Molloy College in Rockville Centre, NY. This Catholic college on Long Island, with an acceptance rate of over 75%, is consistently ranked among the best for its nursing curriculum. In fact, an article in *USA Today* ranked Molloy College #1 as the best U.S. college for a nursing degree, surpassing NYU, U. PENN, and both Villanova and John Hopkins universities.

College bound students seeking a Jesuit education, but lacking the stellar grades and SAT scores required by the likes of Georgetown University and Boston College, should know that they have many potential options. Fairfield University in Fairfield, CT, St. Joseph's University in Philadelphia, PA, University of Scranton in Scranton, PA, and both John Carroll and Xavier universities in Ohio, all have acceptance rates between 71 and 85 percent.

The key, for most students, is to carefully identify the colleges that would be a good match for their talents and interests, and then effectively communicate this information to their colleges of choice. College admissions officers often look kindly upon students who are passionate about their institution and enthusiastic about a particular major that is offered.

Part IV. Filing Successful Applications

Tips for Choosing "Good Fit" Colleges

The key to filing college applications that will attract letters of acceptance is to recognize what the colleges are seeking and then focus the applications accordingly. First and foremost, colleges seek students who are academically prepared to succeed and are motivated to maximize the opportunities offered by the college. A student's GPA is therefore of key importance, since it demonstrates how the student has performed academically in a high school environment. SAT/ACT scores are also critical to most colleges, as they are considered to be the best indication of a student's potential to succeed in a college academic environment. But by the time a student is filing college applications, the GPA and standardized test scores have usually been determined.

Another key criterion for college admissions officers is the determination of what a student will likely contribute to the college community. Is the student a top athlete, a musician, or a student with proven leadership ability? Colleges seek depth of involvement rather than breadth, so students should focus their time and attention on a limited number of activities in which they excel. Colleges are not in the market for well-rounded people, but rather for those with an impressive record of accomplishment in a specific field. By accepting thousands of students who each excel in specific activities, colleges end up with a well-rounded student body.

Once students honestly assess what they have to offer a college community, and what they are seeking out of their college experience, they can choose schools that are a "good fit." Students in search of the perfect college are pretty much all looking for the same thing. First of all, they have to be able to gain acceptance to the college. Secondly, they have to stay in college – hopefully cherishing the experience! Lastly, they have to expect that, upon graduation, their field of study will put them on track for a well paying career.

Time magazine recently went in search of colleges that fit the bill, choosing only colleges that accept at least 66% of applicants. Several colleges within a few hours of New Jersey made the list, including Molloy College, La Salle University, and three Jesuit Universities: St. Joseph's University, Fairfield University and the University of Scranton. All of these colleges also had a high "freshmen retention rate," which is the percentage of freshmen that returned for their sophomore year. And the most popular majors, at all of these colleges, were in fields with high potential career earnings.

Molloy College, a small college in Rockville Centre, NY, was also recognized by *USA Today* as the 4th best college in the U.S. at which to earn a nursing degree. It was topped only by Columbia University, NYU and Georgetown, and ranked higher than the prestigious Johns Hopkins University! Its acceptance rate, last year, was 75% and its retention rate was 89%. To top it off, 65% of the classes had fewer than 20 students and their current annual tuition is only $29,000.

La Salle and St. Joseph's are both popular Philadelphia-area colleges. La Salle reports its most popular majors as Registered Nursing and Marketing/Management. Of the students who applied Early Action to La Salle, 88% were accepted and 75% of freshmen returned for their sophomore year. St. Joseph's is best known for its business majors, including Marketing, Management, Accounting and Finance. Of the students who applied Early Action to St. Joe's, 89% were accepted and 91% of freshmen returned for their sophomore year.

Fairfield University, in the upscale town of Fairfield, CT, is home of the impressive Charles F. Dolan School of Business, School of Engineering, and Marion Peckham Egan School of Nursing and Health Studies. This university, too, favors students who apply early with an Early Decision acceptance rate of 83% and an Early Action acceptance rate of 67%. The school's retention rate is 89%. The University of Scranton in Pennsylvania is most popular for degrees in Biological Sciences, Registered Nursing and Business/ Marketing. Of students who apply Early Action, 84% are accepted and 87% of freshmen return for their sophomore year.

While it's natural for high school students to worry about whether or not they will get accepted to their college of choice, they should realize that college admissions officers worry as well. Their concern is whether or not the students they accept will actually enroll. And their apprehension is well founded, as only 25 colleges in the U.S. enjoy a "yield" (percent of accepted students who actually enroll) of over 50%. These include all eight Ivy League institutions. The only other Northeastern universities in this category are Massachusetts Institute of Technology (MIT) and Yeshiva University in New York. Even such highly acclaimed universities as Johns Hopkins, Lehigh, NYU, and Penn State (University Park campus) have yields that only hover around 33%. Boston College and Syracuse University have even lower yields at 29% and 24% respectively.

In New Jersey, the colleges with the highest yields are NJIT (35%), Rutgers – New Brunswick (33%), Stevens Institute of Technology (32%), The College of New Jersey (29%) and Seton Hall (13%).

Why is there such a gap between the number of students who are accepted and the number who actually enroll? One reason is that a vast number of students are applying to a multitude of colleges. A recent *Forbes* article discussed students applying to 30 to 40 or even more schools. This is feasible due to the existence of the "Common Application" – one application that is accepted at more than 600 colleges and universities. Since students ultimately enroll at only one college, there are a lot of colleges taking a hit to their yield. Another factor is the practice of students applying to one college "early decision" while simultaneously submitting applications to other colleges. If a student is accepted by the "early decision" college, he/she must decline all other acceptances.

Students can use this information to their benefit by showing demonstrated interest to the colleges to which they apply. Colleges all want to boast of the highest yield possible, so it benefits them to accept those students who appear most likely to attend. Students can put themselves in this desirable category by visiting college campuses and signing in, contacting college admissions officers with pertinent questions, and customizing their application essays to demonstrate interest in each particular college to which they are applying. A little personalized attention directed to a college can help a student greatly increase the likelihood of receiving a letter of acceptance.

Advantages of Early Action and Early Decision

Applying "early decision" dramatically increases a student's chance of gaining acceptance to most colleges and universities. The key is for students to do their homework early – researching and visiting colleges and identifying the one that would, hands down, be their top choice. The next step is to apply "early decision," submitting the application by the early decision deadline (typically November 1st or 15th) and signing that you will attend that particular college if accepted.

Colleges are well aware that many students apply to ten or more colleges. But they have no way of knowing for sure which students, if accepted, would actually attend their school. With multi-million dollar annual budgets, it's extremely beneficial for colleges to know which students, if accepted, would definitely be attending (and paying tuition, room, board and fees). Since early decision applications are binding, guaranteeing that accepted students will attend, it's advantageous for colleges to favor these students.

Some highly respected colleges that offer close to a 100% acceptance rate for students who apply early decision include Alfred University in New York and Marlboro College in Vermont. Alfred offers a beautiful, friendly campus, small class sizes, and impressive programs in such fields as art, engineering and equestrian studies. Marlboro, with its student body of fewer than 300 students, boasts an average class size of less than 10 students where a student's course of study is typically self-designed.

Closer to home, Manhattan College, just a few minutes from the George Washington Bridge, offers a 98% acceptance rate to early decision applicants. This Catholic college, with Division I sports, boasts nationally accredited professional schools in Business, Education & Health, and Engineering. Its close proximity to Manhattan provides students with internship opportunities at such prestigious firms as CBS, General Electric, Merrill Lynch, J.P. Morgan and The N.Y. Mets.

If students are ready to commit to one particular college, there are many top institutions that greatly increase the odds of acceptance for early decision applicants. The percentages of students accepted early decision, in comparison to regular decision, are: Lehigh University 63% to 32%, Bucknell University 60% to 28%, Johns Hopkins University 37% to 16%, American University 78% to 44%, Duke University 31% to 11%, Marist College 92% to 36%, and The College of New Jersey 71% to 48%.

Other popular universities and colleges that significantly favor early decision applicants include: Syracuse University, Ithaca College, College of the Holy Cross, Dickinson College, Gettysburg College, Stevens Institute of Technology, and Drew University.

For those students who are turned down by their Early Decision I college, or those who failed to meet the November deadline, all hope is not lost. Many colleges offer Early Decision II, with a January application deadline and notification in February – close to two months prior to the typical April 1st college response date.

New Jersey colleges that offer both Early Decision I and Early Decision II options are: The College of New Jersey, Stevens Institute of Technology, and Drew University.

Colleges in nearby states, popular with New Jersey students, that offer both Early Decision I and II options include: New York University (NYU), Syracuse University, Lehigh University, Bucknell University, Franklin and Marshall College, Gettysburg College, American University and George Washington University.

Students who want to apply to colleges "early," but do not want to limit their options, can apply "early action" to as many colleges as they want that offer the option. The early action application deadline is also typically November 1st or 15th but, if accepted, students are not required to attend.

A recent survey by U.S. News & World Report found that many colleges, both in New Jersey and neighboring states, have a much higher early action acceptance rate than their overall acceptance rate. For example, the University of Connecticut (UConn) reports a 70% early action acceptance rate and a 55% overall acceptance rate. In New Jersey, Monmouth University reports a ratio of 82% to 56%. In Pennsylvania, St. Joseph's University is 95% to 86%, The University of Scranton is 80% to 66%, and Dickinson College is 67% to 44%.

Students who hope to attend an Ivy League school should definitely consider applying under an early plan, as the competition is fierce and only a small proportion of extremely impressive applicants gain admission. Many students who hope to attend an Ivy League school don't really know the differences among these elite institutions. This becomes evident in their applications, lessening their chances of acceptance. So, any student who dreams of an Ivy League education should become well versed on the particular strengths and qualities of each of these eight extremely impressive institutions.

The Ivy League

The "Ivy League" is a consortium of eight of the most elite colleges and universities in the United States: Harvard, Yale, Princeton, Columbia, The University of Pennsylvania, Dartmouth, Brown and Cornell. Academically, they are all extraordinary. They are also among the wealthiest colleges and universities with endowments ranging from $32 billion at Harvard to $2.5 billion at Brown. This translates into extremely generous financial aid offers with most accepted students offered grants (scholarships) rather than loans to cover college costs that hover around $50,000 a year for tuition and fees (without including room and board).

All of these institutions are extremely competitive in the admissions process, all brag of close to 100% graduation rates, and all have a legion of highly successful alumni. But each has its own unique qualities as well.

Harvard, the oldest university in the country, was founded 375 years ago. It is one of the largest of the Ivy League schools (although only 1/3 of its students are undergrads) and hosts 41 varsity sports, which is the most of any Division I school. Its best-known and largest departments are Economics and Government, its best-known alumni include John F. Kennedy, Barack Obama and six other former U.S. presidents, and its best-known dropout is Bill Gates.

Yale attracts one of the most liberal and forward-thinking student bodies in the Ivy League and maintains a strong focus on its undergraduates. Despite its reverence for tradition, it does not have a core curriculum and there are no specific courses required for graduation. Yale alum include three recent U.S. presidents, as well as the current or former presidents of some 70 colleges and universities.

Princeton, one of the smallest of the Ivy League schools, is more conservative than Yale and a third of the size of Harvard. There is a strong focus on a liberal arts education and an emphasis on independent study with a mandatory senior thesis. Princeton students love their "eating clubs" and tend to be more conservative than their Ivy League counterparts.

At Columbia University applications have doubled in the past ten years as its Manhattan location, in the eyes of many students, trumps every other Ivy League city. Students are also drawn to Columbia for its core curriculum, which includes the study of such classics as Homer's *Iliad* and Plato's *Republic* and determines the courses for most of a student's first two years. Proficiency in a foreign language is required, which comes in handy as Columbia offers more than 200 study abroad options.

The University of Pennsylvania (UPenn) stands out among the Ivies for its pre-professional programs, particularly in business (hosting the world-renown Wharton School of Business), engineering and nursing. UPenn established the nation's first medical school, the first journalism curriculum, and the first psychology clinic. It embodies the foresight of it founder, Benjamin Franklin, referred to as the "ultimate visionary and pragmatist."

Dartmouth College, the smallest and most conservative member of the Ivy League, attracts outdoorsy, down-to-earth students who relish the remote, and cold, location in Hanover, NH. The college is known for its cooperative learning atmosphere where students help each other, as opposed to the cutthroat environment at colleges where students are graded on a curve, leaving them in constant competition with their peers. Dartmouth is also know for its "D Plan" of four 10 week terms a year, allowing students to choose any three terms to attend.

Brown University, which continues to be known for its student activism, does *not* emphasize grades, pre-professional programs, or sports. In fact, students are allowed to take an abundance of courses "pass/fail." Many students enjoy the option of doing group independent-study projects, taking courses that they construct primarily by themselves. Always known for its spirit of openness, Brown was the first Ivy to accept students from all religious denominations.

Although it's the easiest Ivy to get into, Cornell University is extremely competitive with the vast majority of courses graded on a curve. It's known for having an extremely hard-working student body, but one that enjoys a great on-campus social life. Its Hotel Administration program is world-renown, and its engineering and architecture programs are likewise highly impressive.

Students seeking an Ivy League education should identify the one that best matches their personality and career aspirations, as their college experience will be very different at each of these unique institutions.

Since numbers don't lie, students with dreams of attending one of the eight prestigious Ivy League colleges/universities should seriously consider applying early. Five of these schools, Brown, Columbia, Cornell, Dartmouth, and The University of Pennsylvania, offer an "Early Decision" plan whereby applicants sign a binding agreement that they will attend if admitted.

Harvard, Princeton, and Yale universities offer a less restrictive form of early application known as "Single Choice Early Action," allowing students to also submit applications to other schools as long as none of their other applications are early action or early decision.

The numbers tell the story as to why students with their heart set on attending a particular Ivy League school should seriously consider filing an early application which typically has a November 1st deadline date. All eight of these elite institutions fill between 43% (Cornell) and 64% (Yale) of their incoming class with Early Decision or Single Choice Early Action applicants. Statistics from the universities' graduating Classes of 2020 and 2021 indicate that the odds of getting accepted by one of these top schools increase dramatically when students sign the binding early application agreement.

Brown University accepted 22% of early applicants but only 8% of regular applicants. Columbia University accepted 19% of early applicants and 5% of regular applicants. The gap was not quite as extreme at Cornell University where 26% of early applicants were accepted, compared to 13% of regular applicants. But the gap was severe at Harvard University where 14% of early applicants were accepted compared to only 3% of regular applicants.

The acceptance numbers at Princeton University were 15% early applicants to 5% for regular applicants. Dartmouth accepted 28% of early and 9% of regular applicants. Yale accepted 17% of early and 4% of regular applicants, and The University of Pennsylvania accepted 22% of early and 7% of regular applicants.

Why is this the scenario, year after year? The Ivy League schools want to maintain their prestigious reputations that are based, in part, on their "yield" – the number of accepted students who enroll at the institution. A great strategy for maintaining a high yield is to fill a large portion of the incoming class with students who, if accepted, will (almost) definitely attend!

Strategies For Getting "You're Accepted" Letter

Students who have their heart set on a particular college are often devastated if they do not receive a thick "acceptance letter" in the mail (or a congratulatory email) full of all the particulars for Accepted Students Day, choosing a dorm, and preparing for all aspects of life on campus.

But sometimes all hope is not lost. Colleges use various tactics to keep their enrollment at peak capacity and their finances in the black. The size of a freshman class typically diminishes as the year progresses, some upper-class students graduate mid-year, and others leave campus to pursue spring semester study abroad opportunities. So many colleges compensate for these empty spots by offering applicants "Second-Semester Admission." Students spend what would have been their freshman fall semester in a variety of ways – studying abroad, taking classes at a local college, or even working to save money – and then move onto their college campus in time for the spring semester.

The University of Maryland, Lehigh University and the University of Southern California are among the many universities that offer some students this option. Closer to home, Fairleigh Dickinson University, in both Teaneck and Madison, N.J., promises admission to a few hundred applicants each year if they first attend, and perform well at, any community college in New Jersey.

Other colleges offer students a delayed acceptance, but make them wait a bit longer to step foot on campus. An option referred to as "Guaranteed Transfer" promises students second or third year admission if they first perform well at another college. Such prestigious schools as Cornell University and Notre Dame University, as well as several colleges in the SUNY (State University of New York) system, utilize this delayed admission tool. Of course, students should never tell a college that they are planning a temporary stay before transferring to the college of their dreams. NYU, for example, is critical of students who enroll for what is ultimately a temporary stay and admits that, in general, it would not admit a student who was not committed to a four year undergraduate experience.

Additionally, some colleges offer "Conditional Admission" whereby a student needs to overcome a particular academic weakness before arriving on campus. Stevens Institute of Technology, for example, requires accepted students who have not yet had calculus to take this course at their local community college in the summer before beginning their college experience. Penn State, likewise, requires certain students who are admitted to their University Park campus to first attend summer school on the campus to hone their academic skills before embarking on their freshman year. College reply letters have become a little cloudier these days – it's not always "accepted" or "denied."

Of course, the best strategy for getting "You're Accepted" letters is to submit finely honed applications. Remember, your application gets just a few minutes of attention from a college admission officer. Sloppy or incomplete applications make a bad impression. Spelling and grammar count, as an application filed with errors indicates that either the applicant doesn't have the writing skills necessary to succeed in college, or the applicant simply doesn't care. Missing SAT scores, recommendation letters, or high school transcripts will get an application put aside and possibly not reviewed again until many fewer seats are available. Students should have one or two people carefully proofread their applications, before submitting, to check for any errors or missing information. Likewise, students should be sure that all materials required from outside sources (College Board SAT scores, teacher recommendation letters, counselor transcripts) are all sent on a timely basis.

Students should be sure that the list of colleges to which they are applying is a logical one based on their high school grades, SAT scores, and field of interest. Information is readily available as to the average high school GPA and standardized test scores of accepted students at every college. While it's fine to have a few "reach" schools on the list, it's also important to apply to colleges where a student's high school record indicates that he/she would academically make the cut. Also, if a student indicates a career interest as an engineer, architect, or teacher, for example, it's important to verify in advance that the college offers a degree in the intended field.

Why should the college accept you? While a college will likely *not* ask this question so directly, it's exactly what an admissions officer is thinking while reading your application. Teens who highlight the talents, qualities, and potential they will bring to a college campus are *much* more likely to gain acceptance. There are many opportunities on a college application for students to present this information. It can be showcased on the "Activities" section of an application, enumerated on an attached resume, and written about in the application essay. Colleges are looking to populate their campus with a well-rounded student body, encompassing students with a wide range of interests, talents and accomplishments. Be sure to let the college know how you would be an attribute to their community!

Most importantly, show demonstrated interest. As previously mentioned, colleges are well aware that most college-bound students apply to many institutions. While students are worried about getting rejected by colleges, the colleges are just as concerned about getting rejected by the students to whom they issue offers of acceptance. So colleges, when evaluating an application, carefully consider the likelihood that the student, if accepted, would actually attend. Students should therefore make every effort to actually visit all the colleges to which they are applying, and then personalize each application to let each college know what specifically appeals to them and why that college is a "perfect fit."

A recent New York Times *Education Life* supplement featured a cover stating, "Admissions is unfair: Here's why." Surrounding the cynical title were clues as to the criteria that might swing a college applicant to the acceptance or rejection pile.

Before slumping into a depression, college bound students should take comfort from the fact that 87% of colleges accept at least half of their applicants. It's the world famous institutions that, each year, collectively reject hundreds of thousands of students who could actually thrive at their schools. This scenario plays out not only at all of the prestigious Ivy League colleges and universities, but also at other popular institutions. UCLA received more than 100,000 applications for about 6,000 seats in this year's freshmen class. The acceptance rate was less than 10% at the University of Chicago, M.I.T, Duke, Johns Hopkins, Notre Dame and the University of Southern California.

What college-bound students need to do, therefore, is be aware of the criteria that college admissions officers are taking under careful consideration. Some of these benchmarks are outside a student's control. Many of the top colleges favor "legacy" students – those with an alumni parent. Many colleges give preference to "first generation" students – those whose parents do not have a college education. Many colleges value geographical diversity – seeking a freshmen class that represents all 50 states and as many foreign countries as possible. According to a recent report by the National Association for College Admission Counseling, about half of all colleges and universities indicated that an applicant's ability to pay played a role in their admissions decision. If students can use any of these criteria to their benefit, they should highlight the information in their applications.

Of course, high school grades, the rigor of a student's course load, and SAT/ACT scores still carry the most weight in the admissions process. Most colleges believe that students' grades and standardized test scores are the best indicators in predicting the likelihood of their success in college.

Again, it can't be stressed enough that demonstrated interest is of key importance. Colleges do not want to get turned down by the students whom they accept as this lowers their "yield" and, ultimately, their reputation. They carefully assess the likelihood of whether a student, if accepted, would actually enroll at their school. The strongest expression of demonstrated interest is for a student to apply "early decision" to a college. This assures the college that, if accepted, the student will actually enroll. Colleges also look favorably on students who interact with them in a number of ways: campus visits, contact with an admissions officer, or response to an email.

It's important for students to go into the college application process with their eyes wide open, aware of the assets that they can use to their benefit and diligent enough to present themselves in the best possible light.

The Common App

Back in 1975, administrators from fifteen colleges got together and decided to create one application that students could use to apply to any or all of their colleges. This was the birth of "The Common App" which is now accepted by more than 600 colleges and universities across the United States and greatly simplifies the college application process for the estimated 21 million students who attend an American college or university each year.

The Common App is an online application that asks a series of questions in several categories, including: parents' educational history and current employment, students' SAT/ACT/AP test scores, senior year courses, high school activities, and intended college major. There is also an essay of 250 to 650 words that is required by the majority of Common App colleges.

On the "dashboard" of the Common App, students list all of the colleges to which they want to apply. Most colleges have some additional questions, and some even have supplemental essays (although they are usually only looking for 100 to 250 words). Once all of the questions are answered and essays are completed, students pay the application fee for each college online, and press "submit."

Students must also provide their high school guidance counselor with a list of the colleges to which they are applying so the counselors can forward their transcripts and recommendation letters. Many high schools use the software program *Naviance* for this purpose.

The good news for New Jersey students who want to attend college in state is that all Garden State colleges and universities, with four exceptions, accept the Common App. The exceptions are: Rutgers, Montclair State, and Thomas Edison State universities and Berkeley College. Other colleges and universities, popular with New Jersey students, that accept The Common App include: The University of Delaware, The University of Maryland, George Washington University and Catholic University of America in Washington D.C., Fairfield and Quinnipiac universities in Connecticut, Fordham, Marist and NYU in New York, and Drexel, Temple, and St. Joseph's universities in Pennsylvania.

Schools that feature their own application, most notably state universities such as Penn State schools and University of California schools, ask many of the same questions that students will have answered on their Common App. So filling out the Common App is the best starting point for students in the college application process.

The Common App "goes live" on August 1st of each year. This means that the updated application, that will be used for the upcoming academic year, appears online. The good news is that students can start filling out the Common App earlier than August 1st of the summer they are heading into their senior year, as almost all of the information they input is rolled over to the new application. After August 1st, students should read through their application and fill in any answers that did not roll over, as some questions change each year so there will likely be some questions that will need to be addressed.

The Essay

The acceptance of a high school senior by five Ivy League schools, as well as Stanford University, gained national attention.   But it wasn't the student's stellar grades, impressive SAT scores, or remarkable academic accomplishments that caught the world's attention.   It was her essay!

Brittany Stinson of Wilmington, Delaware wrote about Costco. She relayed anecdotes of her Costco visits from the time she was a two-year-old right through her teenage years. She shared her awe of the store that she labeled "the apex of consumerism" and wondered aloud of the incomprehensible shopping habits of fellow patrons with "carts piled with frozen burritos, cheese puffs, tubs of ice cream, and weight loss supplements." She shared how the kingdom of Costco led her to "explore beyond the bounds of rational thought."

What can the millions of college-bound students learn from this story?   The Costco essay personifies what college admissions officers are truly looking for in a college application essay.   They want a student's personality to shine through. They want there to be a creative angle. They want honesty to seep through the essay.

One of the most popular Common Application essay questions, and the one used by Brittany, states, "Some students have a background, identity, interest, or talent that is so meaningful they believe their application would be incomplete without it. If this sounds like you, then please share your story."

This essay prompt gives students carte blanche to be creative and honest as they share their own personal story. A student might open with an anecdote, which can immediately engage the reader. This mini-story should be revealing of the student's personality and character and launch the essay into a revelation of who the student is today and what the student's vision is of the future. The very general nature of this question allows students to share a story or situation from their home life, school, work, favorite activity, religious celebration, or anything at all, and describe its impact on their life and the person they are today.

The essay topic chosen by Brittany is the first of seven options offered on the Common App. Here are the other six, although students should note that while the overall topics tend to stay the same, the wording of a few essay questions may vary a bit from one year to the next.

Essay #2.   *The lessons we take from obstacles we encounter can be fundamental to later success. Recount a time when you faced a challenge, setback, or failure. How did it affect you, and what did you learn from the experience?*

Essay #3.   *Reflect on a time when you questioned or challenged a belief or idea. What prompted your thinking? What was the outcome?*

Essay #4. *Describe a problem you've solved or a problem you'd like to solve. It can be an intellectual challenge, a research query, an ethical dilemma – anything that is of personal importance, no matter the scale. Explain its significance to you and what steps you took or could be taken to identify a solution.*

Essay #5. *Discuss an accomplishment, event, or realization that sparked a period of personal growth and a new understanding of yourself or others.*

Essay #6. *Describe a topic, idea, or concept you find so engaging that it makes you lose all track of time. Why does it captivate you? What or who do you turn to when you want to learn more?*

Essay #7. *Share an essay on any topic of your choice. It can be one you've already written, one that responds to a different prompt, or one of your own design.*

Colleges look to the essay to envision the personality of each applicant. The essay is the main opportunity for an applicant to share his/her life story – sharing human qualities that are not otherwise apparent in the application. Students should think carefully about the information they want to share with colleges that is not evident on other parts of their application, and then choose an essay topic that allows them to do so.

Due to the importance of writing an interesting, grammatically correct essay, most students get help from a variety of sources. In many schools, the writing of the Common App essay is incorporated into the English IV curriculum with teachers editing their students' rough drafts. Often parents, relatives or friends offer their input as well. At times, a private counselor is hired to insure that an impressive essay is submitted that is likely to garner the approval of college admissions officers. The end result, according to colleges, is that most of the essays they receive are good enough to be published. The problem: they seldom reflect the students' independent work.

Colleges often get a better idea of an applicant's natural writing ability and suitability for admission through the use of a supplemental essay. Many colleges, including almost all of the most competitive institutions, require one or more supplemental essays addressing specific questions. Often the topic revolves around why the student is applying to that particular college, allowing the admissions team to assess the student's interest in, and potential match for, their institution. NYU's supplemental essay, personifying this strategy, states: *We would like to know more about your interest in NYU. We are particularly interested in knowing what motivated you to apply to NYU and more specifically, why you have applied or expressed interest in a particular campus, school, college, program, and/or area of study?*

Colleges also utilize the shorter supplemental questions to envision the personality of each applicant. Students should use this opportunity to share their human qualities that are not apparent in other parts of the application and to personalize their answers. If asked, "Whom do you admire?" students should avoid the urge to write about Martin Luther King or Abraham Lincoln and tell about a person who has impacted them in a more personal manner. If asked, "What is a book that you love?" students should skip *War and Peace* and other works of the world's most renown authors and share a book they are particularly passionate about or one that has influenced them in a profound manner.

Students should also utilize supplemental essays as a chance to demonstrate their interest in a particular college, and should specifically state the programs, courses, internships, study abroad opportunities, and any other characteristics that make the institution a perfect match for their college ambitions. Students should exercise care to insure that this essay is well written, grammatically correct, and offers information that is not evident in other parts of their application. Just because it's not the main essay of the application, and is not the focus of outside scrutiny by teachers and parents, doesn't mean that it's not just as important to colleges.

Study Abroad Opportunities

Almost every college and university offers its students the opportunity to study abroad as it provides an ideal experience to help them expand their horizons and become more open-minded, educated citizens of our global community. Students, in their college applications, should express an interest in studying abroad and should specify where they would ideally like to go and how they would maximize the experience. Since colleges are seeking intellectually curious students who will make the most of their opportunities, the college application is the perfect place for students to demonstrate interest in each particular college by citing the specific study abroad options they find most appealing.

So where are students heading? Of the more than 300,000 students who study abroad for academic credit each year, more than half are choosing a European country. The United Kingdom takes first place each year, with the key attraction being English as the national language. According to the most recent data from the Institute of International Education, Italy, Spain and France take 2nd, 3rd, and 4th place, respectively. They are followed by China, the only non-European country in the top five. Rounding out the top twelve countries, in order of popularity, are Germany, Ireland, Costa Rica, Australia, Japan, South Africa and India.

While students attending almost any U.S. college have the opportunity to study abroad, it is particularly encouraged at certain colleges and universities in the area. The University of Delaware, which launched America's first study abroad program back in 1923, offers students the opportunity to study on any of six continents. (The University does not currently offer a program in Antarctica.)

Study abroad is likewise extremely popular at several Pennsylvania colleges and universities. At Dickinson College nearly 70% of students, and 40% of the faculty, participate in study abroad programs. Its Global Mosaics program allows students to take semester-long courses on campus and then travel abroad to partake in fieldwork or immersion work. At Gettysburg College more than 95% of its students participate in one of the Center for Global Education programs, which partners with over 50 countries. At Susquehanna University students are actually required to participate in the Global Opportunities program. They have the option of a short or long semester, and a choice of locations around the world including such natural wonders as the Galapagos Islands and Andes Mountains.

Colleges typically charge students the same fees for international study that they would pay if remaining on their home campus, eliminating financial obstacles for those who want to experience the world.

Hundreds of thousands of college students each year recognize that the opportunity to become immersed in another culture for months at a time is something that may not happen for them again in their lifetime!

The Art of the Interview

A Harvard University junior gained a lot of attention for being offered internships with some of the most sought after companies: Facebook, Google, Apple, Microsoft, Goldman Sachs and Morgan Stanley. When asked the secrets of her success, she claimed that being prepared for interview questions was very important.

To one of the most common questions, "What would you like to tell me about yourself," she offered some guidelines. She recommended that students start off with a brief introduction including their name, college, and field of study. Next, students should mention a few of their accomplishments of which they are most proud. Lastly, students should state the reasons they want to work at the particular company and share the talents and skills they possess that would be relevant for the position they are seeking. Basically, the interviewee should let the interviewer know how the company would benefit from having him/her onboard.

Students should always plan exactly what they will say when asked the most common interview questions. This is vital, whether interviewing with a prospective college, or with a company for an internship or full time job. What are some of the most frequently asked questions?

According to Glassdoor.com, a popular jobs and recruiting site, interviewees should be prepared to answer: What are your strengths and weaknesses? Where do you see yourself in five or ten years? What can you offer us that someone else cannot? Tell me about an accomplishment you are most proud of. Tell me about a time you made a mistake. What is your dream job?

At an interview with a college admissions officer, a student might likely be asked why they think the college is a "good fit" and what attributes they would bring to the campus. By preparing their answers well in advance, and practicing their delivery skills – either in front of a mirror or to a friend or family member – students will enter their interviews feeling well prepared and confident and have the best chance of a successful outcome.

Still, almost everyone dreads the interviewing process, especially when there is a lot at stake. As previously mentioned, students should certainly practice in advance answering common questions, such as, "Why should we select you?" "What experience would you bring with you?" and "What are your proudest accomplishments?" It's easy to remember the good things we've done, and we're usually proud to talk about our assets and achievements.

Things get trickier when the interviewer asks a question such as, "Can you tell me about a time when you failed?" There is even an essay prompt on the *Common Application* that focuses on failure. It states, "The lessons we take from obstacles we encounter can be fundamental to later success. Recount a time when you faced a challenge, setback, or failure. How did it affect you, and what did you learn from the experience?"

The worse thing students can do is pretend they've never failed at anything. Is it possible for anyone to have lived through their childhood, and many of their teen years, and never have struggled in an academic subject, been cut from a sports team, lost a school election, or suffered any setback? If this is so, in the eyes of the interviewer the student might be a risky choice because no one knows how he or she will handle the inevitable setback or failure that is sure to loom in the future.

Most likely, the interviewee is simply trying to put his/her best foot forward. But it's a mistake to think that admitting to a past failure is a sign of weakness. It's actually an opportunity for a student to demonstrate that a lesson was learned, and he/she has moved on from the failure. People who think they have never failed at anything either don't have the self-awareness to recognize their weaknesses, or the self-confidence to admit to their failures. Either way, coming off as pompous in an interview is a turn-off that is not likely to turn out well.

Another mistake interviewees sometimes make is to talk in too casual a manner and use inappropriate language when answering questions. It is never acceptable to refer, in an offensive way, to another person based on race, gender, or any other defining quality. Interviewers want to identify candidates who will represent their college in a non-biased, respectable manner.

In short, students should present themselves in the best possible light, while being honest and realistic when answering questions – even about their flaws.

Summary of Key Strategies

Time is the greatest gift that future college-bound students can give themselves. The qualities and accomplishments that colleges are seeking in their future students are *not* ones that can be achieved in senior year of high school alone. Six strategies for acing your college applications are:

1) *The earlier you start, the better.* This advice is all encompassing. You want to get great grades right from your first semester of high school, as each grade contributes towards your overall grade point average (G.P.A.) You should start taking the SAT early in your high school years, as you can take the test as many times as you want and then submit your highest scores. Practice may *not* make perfect, but the more often you take this all-important test the more comfortable you will become with it and the more knowledgeable about exactly what you need to know. And it's never too early to start thinking about potential careers as it's ideal to have a chosen major when the time to fill out college applications rolls around.

2) *Recognize that colleges are looking for well-rounded student bodies, **not** well-rounded students.* Earlier generations of college-bound students were encouraged to become renaissance people and join many clubs, participate in sports, hold jobs, and do volunteer work as well. Colleges have since realized that this is contrary to what they should be looking for. They don't need thousands of students who were minimally involved in a gamut of activities. Colleges now want students who have chosen a specific area of interest -- a sport, club, activity or cause – and made a substantial impact.

3) *Do your homework.* There are more than 3,000 colleges in the U.S. alone. Many colleges are incredibly strong in a particular field of study, but just average in other academic areas. Students need to carefully research colleges to find ones that are the "best fit" for their academic needs, and also meet their preferences in areas such as geographical location, campus setting, travel abroad and internship opportunities, cost, and a host of other criteria.

4) *Demonstrate interest.* Every college is greatly concerned with its "yield" — the percent of accepted students who actually enroll. So the best strategy to actually gain acceptance is to convince the college/university that you will almost certainly attend if given the opportunity to do so. If at all possible, be sure to visit any college to which you are applying, sign in so the college has a record of your visit, and take notes of the college's specific qualities that make it so appealing. In your application essay, be sure to include a paragraph stating specifically why that particular college is the ideal one for you.

5) *Get top grades and SAT (or ACT) scores.* Give colleges every reason to accept you. You are going to college for an education, and the best indicators of your strength as a student are your G.P.A. and your standardized test scores. These are also the criteria that will be used in determining your scholarship offers, so it's wise for so many reasons to put serious time and effort into presenting impressive grades and scores.

6) *Recognize that optional really isn't optional.* If colleges ask for something – even if they say it's optional – do it, and do it to the best of your ability. This advice is also pertinent for the "optional" essay section of the SAT. Realize that other applicants – your competitors – will be doing everything suggested by the colleges, and you certainly don't want to be at a disadvantage.

The End of the Road

April 1st is a special day for college-bound students. It's the deadline day for most colleges to let students know whether or not they've been accepted. Now the ball is in the student's court! Many students find themselves with a pile of acceptance letters (or emails). How should students make this pivotal decision?

First of all, remember the purpose of college. It's certainly intended to make students more educated, in general, and more aware of the world and the issues surrounding them. But, more pragmatically, most students attend college with the goal of preparing for a career that will support them for the rest of their lives. So the best choice college is often the one with the strongest program in a student's intended field of study. A little research will reveal the mid-career salary of alumni from each of the colleges under consideration, as well as the acceptance rate to medical and dental schools, law schools and graduate programs.

Finances also come into play in the decision of most students. But students should realize that the financial aid "package" offered by any particular college can often be negotiated. If a student's dream college offers less money than another to which the student has been accepted, there's no harm in contacting the admissions office at the preferred college and requesting that the grant money (the "scholarship" portion that does not get paid back) be reconsidered. Let the #1 college know of the other, better offers.

Students typically do not have to make the big decision until May 1st. So they should take advantage of the "Accepted Students Day" offered by all of the colleges they are considering. This is the perfect opportunity for students to get another feel for each college, ask any questions that are still on their minds, and consider all aspects of each school, including the food, dorms, activities, campus, and surrounding community. Usually, after doing their research and visiting each campus (one or more times), students have a good sense of which college is the "right fit" for the exciting years that lie ahead.

But sometimes, things do not go as expected or hoped for. If April 1st has rolled around and a student has not gained admission to a college of choice, all is not lost. The National Association for College Admission Counseling (NACAC) releases a list, in early May of each year, of colleges that still have room for students seeking admission for the upcoming fall semester. May 1st is the national response deadline for most colleges in the U.S. By that date, students must choose the college they will be attending in the fall and send in a deposit to reserve their seat (and room and board, if they are planning to live on campus). Since most students apply to a multitude of colleges, it's impossible for colleges to know for sure how many students will actually enroll until the reply deadline rolls around. After May 1st, colleges that have not met their target enrollment are anxious to accept additional students in order to bring in the tuition money necessary to keep on budget.

Often, even well-qualified students are not accepted to the college of their dreams. Other times, students change their minds. As the time to leave home for college approaches, students sometimes wish they had chosen a school closer to home. For these reasons and others (basic procrastination!), students may find themselves approaching high school graduation without a plan for the fall.

Fortunately for these students, the list that the NACAC releases each May typically includes more than 400 colleges that are still accepting applications for the upcoming fall semester. Last May, the list included ten New Jersey colleges and universities that had openings for both incoming freshmen and transfer students and were still offering housing and financial aid. The public NJ universities were New Jersey Institute of Technology, Stockton University, and William Patterson University. The private NJ schools were Bloomfield College, the College of Saint Elizabeth, and Caldwell, Drew, Georgian Court, Rider, and Saint Peter's universities.

There were also 42 colleges and universities in Pennsylvania still accepting applications, including Duquesne, LaSalle, St. Joseph's, Susquehanna, and Penn State universities, The University of Scranton, Ursinus College, and York College of Pennsylvania.

Students seeking a New York education found seats still available at 40 schools including The Culinary Institute of America, The New School, Manhattan College, and Adelphi, Hofstra and St. John's universities. Students wanting to spread their wings were happy to find some colleges still accepting applications in Australia, Canada and the United Kingdom.

Of course, it is not ideal to still be applying to colleges in May of senior year. But if that is the situation, it is vital to act promptly. Students who are interested in any particular college should immediately contact its admissions department to find out exactly what materials need to be submitted. Students should also inquire about the availability of merit-based and need-based financial aid. After meeting all requirements, as quickly as possible, students should follow-up with an admissions officer and reiterate their strong desire to attend that particular college. An acceptance letter may appear in their mail (or email) sooner than they expect!

Part V. Finances, Scholarships, Avoiding College Debt

What Students Can Do Ahead of Time

The very best scenario is for students to avoid, or at least minimize, their college debt. There are several things that student can do to make this a reality.

While in high school, students should seek part-time jobs with companies that may later contribute to their college expenses. These companies include: AT&T, Bank of American, Best Buy, BP, Comcast, Disney, Verizon, Wegmans, Starbucks and UPS.

High school students should take their studies very seriously, as the financial cost of starting college academically unprepared can be astronomical. According to the National Assessment of Educational Progress (NAEP), which issues the Nation's Report Card, only about a third of U.S. high school seniors are prepared for college level coursework in Math and Reading. Lack of readiness for college is a major culprit in low graduation rates, as the majority of students who begin college in remedial courses never complete their degrees. To add insult to injury, these students frequently accumulate substantial student debt that must be paid back whether or not they ultimately graduate.

Studies have shown that anywhere from 28% to 40% of all undergraduate students enroll in at least one remedial course. This is a course they need to pay for, attend, complete assignments for, and pass, but for which they do not get any college credit. This is often frustrating and expensive for students and, if several remedial courses are required, can considerably lengthen the number of years it takes to graduate. Often students find that the best remedy to this dilemma is to take any necessary remedial courses at their local community college, which typically has the lowest tuition fees, while living at home. By not enrolling in a four-year college until academically ready to take courses for credit, students can greatly minimize their student debt and increase their chances of graduating "on time."

Most college freshmen arrive on campus with the intention of donning their graduation cap and gown four years later. But statistics show that this actually happens for fewer than half of New Jersey college students. According to NJ.com, the percentage of freshmen who go on to earn their bachelors degree in four years or less is 90% at Princeton, 73% at The College of New Jersey, 61% at Centenary College, and 59% at Rutgers (New Brunswick). Most other New Jersey colleges, both public and private, have four-year graduation rates lower than 50%. These include Bloomfield College at 6%, New Jersey City University at 7%, and Felician, Kean and William Patterson, all at under 20%. Colleges at or below 40% include Rutgers (both Camden and Newark campuses), Fairleigh Dickinson (metro campus), Montclair State, Saint Peter's, and Stevens Institute of Technology.

One way for high school students to increase their chances of earning a college degree in four years (or less) is to take college courses while still in high school, earning credits that will likely transfer to their future college. Students who are academically able should take as many AP (Advanced Placement) courses as possible during their high school years. The curriculum for these courses is written by The College Board, the same company that produces the SAT exam. Students who take an AP course, and the corresponding exam in May of the academic year, are usually given credit by their future college if they earn a score of 4 or 5.

AP courses are offered in more than 30 subjects, including: Art History, Studio Art, Music Theory, English Language & Composition, English Literature & Composition, U.S. History, European History, World History, Macroeconomics, Microeconomics, Psychology, Calculus, Statistics, Computer Science, Biology, Chemistry, Physics, Environmental Science, Spanish, French, German, Italian, Latin, Chinese and Japanese.

The *Washington Post* recently touted a program that utilizes AP courses to help rein in student debt. It's called "Freshman Year for Free," and it's offered through the Modern States Education Alliance, a non-profit that helps students get through college with substantially less debt. The way it works is that anyone -- including high school students -- can take online courses that prepare them to pass Advanced Placement (AP) and College Level Examination Program (CLEP) tests. Students who score well on these tests can earn enough college credits to bypass their freshman year and start college as sophomores -- saving 25% of tuition costs and a year of their lives!

To make this even more financially attractive, textbooks and materials are free. Modern States Education Alliance is even giving out vouchers to the first 10,000 test takers to cover exam fees. The College Board currently charges $92 for each AP exam and $85 for each CLEP test. (If they are out of vouchers, high school guidance counselors can often get fee waivers for financially strapped high school students.)

This is a great opportunity for students to take courses offered by professors at many of the most elite colleges and universities. The program's freshman-level courses include some taught by professors at Columbia, NYU, Rutgers, MIT, Berkeley, Johns Hopkins, Boston University and George Washington University. The courses prepare students to pass AP and CLEP exams that are accepted, for credit, by more than 2,900 universities. Students are not limited as to the number of courses they can take. The courses are self-paced, which is an asset to many students. But they should keep in mind the timing of the exams that must be passed (with certain scores) in order to earn college credits. CLEP tests can be taken year-round, but AP exams are only offered on specific dates in May of each year. Registration for this program is at www.modernstates.org. It can be quite the resume booster for a college-bound student to highlight "acing" a college level course taken with an Ivy League professor!

Another option for students, while still in high school, is to start amassing college credits by taking courses (at very affordable rates) at their local community college. Or, they can take courses online at sites such as edx.org or coursera.org where the choice of courses is almost limitless!

Students should also take the SAT exam very seriously, and put considerable time and energy into getting the highest scores that they are able. Students are allowed to take the SAT exam as many times as they like and then, when applying to college, they can send their highest scores. Many colleges allow students to "superscore," which means they can send their highest Math score from one SAT sitting and their highest Evidence-based Reading & Writing score from another SAT sitting. Since most colleges award scholarship money based on SAT scores, the easiest and most productive way for students to minimize their student debt is to maximize their SAT scores. Students should realize that whatever scholarship money they are awarded for their freshman year is typically renewed for the following three years. So if, by earning impressive SAT scores, a student is offered a $10,000 merit award, that would turn into $40,000 over the course of four years.

When finances are a serious issue, students can also consider taking a "gap year" before beginning college. Students should apply to their colleges of choice as high school seniors and, when accepted, ask to have their admission deferred for a year. Almost all colleges are happy to oblige. Students can then work for a year, ear-marking their earnings toward their future college costs while gaining insight into the career they hope to pursue.

Avoiding Massive College Debt

When talking about college debt, the statistics are never encouraging. In fact, the story gets sadder each year. The average recent college graduate has amassed a debt exceeding $35,000 and joins the ranks of 44 million borrowers who collectively owe $1.3 trillion in education debt. The key is to avoid being a part of this grim statistic. A college education is too costly a venture for most students to enter into without a clear sense of purpose. Likewise, students should realize that there are many roads to the same destination – some much more expensive than others.

Students should avoid starting college "undecided" regarding a choice of major. There are two pitfalls here. The first is that, once a student does choose a major, many of the courses previously taken may not be part of the required course curriculum. Hence, the student will often have to spend an additional semester, year, or even longer at college. Secondly, at many colleges, students who were admitted "undecided" have to apply to be admitted into their major of choice. If rejected, they have to transfer to a different college or pursue a major that may not be to their liking. The longer it takes to acquire a college degree the longer the costs add up!

Another advantage of identifying, before starting college, the academic field they wish to pursue is that students can then carefully research appropriate scholarships. Hundreds of scholarships are available to students seeking an education in the STEM (Science, Technology, Engineering, Math) fields. The SMART Scholarship, for example, is offered by the Department of Defense (DOD) and provides full tuition and a stipend to students in STEM willing to work for the DOD upon graduation.

In addition to seeking scholarships based on their major, students should search for scholarships for any characteristics specific to them. There are scholarships for: under-represented minorities, women seeking traditionally male-oriented careers, legacy students attending the alma mater of a parent, first-in-family to attend college, commitment to community service, and, of course, talent – be it in music, art, writing, athletics, or a host of other areas.

When choosing potential colleges, high school students should not necessarily reach for the stars – unless it's to a college with an impressive endowment that is generous with scholarship money. Students will find that if they apply to a college that is a tier below the level of school to which they could likely get accepted, the scholarship money will almost certainly be much greater.

Students planning to major in business, for example, often seek to gain acceptance to NYU's Stern School of Business. The cost of attending this impressive college hovers around $70,000 a year for tuition, fees, room and board. This does not include costs for books, supplies, health insurance, transportation, and other expenses.

Students able to gain acceptance to NYU could reasonably expect to be welcomed at St. John's University in New York, St. Joseph's University in Philadelphia, and a host of other institutions with impressive business schools, substantially lower costs of attendance, and generous merit money (to attract strong students) – which does *not* get paid back.

Students should seriously consider the cost of attending comparable colleges. While The College of New Jersey (TCNJ), Villanova, Drexel and LaSalle are all highly regarded schools in relatively close proximity to each other, the cost of attending each may vary dramatically. New Jersey students get "in-state" tuition at TCNJ. Drexel and LaSalle universities are known to be much more generous with scholarships than Villanova.

Students should always consider applying to an in-state public college, which typically offers the lowest tuition costs, and, if possible, should think about commuting. At most four-year public universities, the cost of room and board is more than the cost of tuition! At Rutgers University in New Brunswick, for example, the 2017-18 cost of in-state tuition and fees is $14,638 while the cost of room, board and expenses is $16,203. If living at home is not an option, students should look into becoming a Resident Advisor (RA) as they would be paid a stipend and also receive free housing and, often, free board as well.

Once students are enrolled in college they should live simply, minimizing their expenses and use any extra money to pay down student debt before it even comes due. While it might be tempting to charge spring break to a credit card, no one wants to be paying it off, with interest, years after the memories have faded. Students should also take advantage of work-study opportunities on campus to earn their spending money – so they won't add credit card debt to student loan debt. Part-time jobs are also a great source of income that can be directed toward college expenses. Ideally, students should seek jobs with companies that feature tuition assistance programs for part-time employees, such as Verizon Wireless, UPS and Starbucks. It's great to get part of your tuition paid while earning a paycheck as well!

A great way for students to save money while in college is to take advantage of the multitude of discounts available to those with a college ID. Almost every industry wants to attract college students, not just for their immediate buying power but also for their business later in life when they are earning serious incomes. So companies that focus on travel, technology, entertainment, books, cell phones, insurance, retail sales and food, as well as many other products, often offer significant discounts to those who can flash a college ID.

By visiting the website www.studentadvantage.com and signing up for a card, students can save money in a vast array of industries. For example, traveling discounts include 10% on Amtrak, up to 20% on Alamo and National car rentals, and 20% on Greyhound bus fares. Entertainment discounts include up to 40% off pre-paid tickets at AMC Theatres and up to 25% at Cinemark Cinemas. Retail discounts at greatly varying rates are offered at such popular online sites as ChampsSports.com, FootLocker.com, Footaction.com, Target.com, and RiteAid.com.

Technology is always important to college students. Among the companies that offer impressive savings are Apple, Adobe, Microsoft, Lenovo and Sony. Students can use their devices to download The New York Times for free or The Wall Street Journal for $1 per week. Since few (if any) students are without a cell phone, it also makes good financial sense for them to check out the student discounts offered by Verizon Wireless, AT&T and Sprint.

When it comes time for entertainment, the very best discounts are those offered at sporting events right on campus where students pay a fraction of the price charged to the general public. For major league teams the discounts vary by city, but many offer student specials including the New York Yankees and Mets, Philadelphia Phillies and New Jersey Devils.

Some retail stores that offer discounts to the college crowd include: J. Crew, The Limited, Eastern Mountain Sports, Champ Sports, Banana Republic, Ann Taylor, Levi's, Club Monaco and Alex & Ani.

Discounts at restaurants and bars vary greatly by location. Some national chains that sometimes offer student discounts include Subway, Pizza Hut, Papa John's, Dairy Queen and Burger King. In addition, there are many regional or independent eateries near most campuses where students should ask about discounts.

The college years are an ideal time to take advantage of discounts offered by companies hoping to make students into life-long customers!

There are other effective financial strategies that are appropriate for many students. Students who are interested in a military career can join ROTC and have some, or all, of their college costs covered in exchange for their participation in ROTC on campus during their college years and a commitment to active duty afterwards.

Students who are interested in studying abroad – for *all* of their college years – will find tuitions much more affordable in Canada and the United Kingdom (where courses will still be taught in English). In the United Kingdom, undergraduate programs are typically three years long, offering another opportunity to save money.

After graduation, when college debt payments start coming due, it's wise to pay off the loans with the highest interest rates first. Also, there is typically a small interest rate reduction offered to those who opt to make monthly payments via direct deposit.

Some lucky students who take a job with the federal government may be eligible to have their student loans forgiven after they have been employed for ten years. Similar programs exist in some areas for teachers who work in impoverished neighborhoods.

Regardless of each student's individual circumstances and situation, the key is to think seriously about finances before heading off to college as the repercussions of educational debt can be life-changing. College graduates often find it impossible to launch independent lives – buying a home, starting a family, saving for retirement – when a large chunk of their paychecks are earmarked to repay their college loans. Living frugally in the short run -- by minimizing expenses and borrowing the least amount possible -- may allow graduates to live lavishly later on!

Best Colleges for Your Money

Americans search *Google* using the words "college" and "value" more than a million times a month, according to Money magazine. The reason is most likely anxiety over the staggering cost of college. Parents and students wanting to get the best value for their substantial investment of time and money are smart to do some research. Studies undertaken annually by companies such as Kiplinger and Money consistently find that the best value for the money is to attend a state university or a prestigious, well-endowed private college or university.

According to a recent report by Kiplinger on the best values among public colleges, the top ranking schools are: (#1) The University of North Carolina at Chapel Hill, (#2) University of Virginia and (#3) University of Florida. These are followed by state universities in California, Michigan, Virginia, Wisconsin, Maryland and Georgia. The problem is that most public universities are only a great value for families who reside in the state. For example, the annual cost for an out-of-state student to attend UNC-Chapel Hill is $45,494, while an in-state student with need-based aid pays $6,332.

The College of New Jersey ranks 23rd among Kiplinger's best value public colleges in the U.S. with an average annual cost of $16,265 for New Jersey students after need-based aid. Rutgers University in New Brunswick ranks 43rd with an average annual cost of $14,581 for New Jersey students after need-based aid. (Cost is one of many criteria in determining "best value.")

When private colleges and universities are evaluated, Princeton University ranks high on everyone's list. Kiplinger ranked it first, while Money ranked it third. The reason is that Princeton meets 100% of each student's financial need. At Princeton, borrowing isn't a part of the financial aid package; all aid is awarded in the form of scholarships and grants. No one is expected to take out loans. Of course the catch is that very few New Jersey students are accepted to Princeton University, which admits only 7% of its applicants.

The same is true of almost all private, "best value" colleges, which include: Massachusetts Institute of Technology (M.I.T.) with an acceptance rate of 8%, Stanford University with an acceptance rate of 6%, and Harvard University with an acceptance rate of 6%. So while it's great news that these elite "best value" colleges allow students to graduate virtually debt-free, the bad news is that hardly anyone can get into them!

New Jersey students seeking an affordable college education often assume that the best route is to choose an in-state public college or university. While it's a great option to consider attending one of New Jersey's eleven public colleges, it's not the only way to go.

Some of the highest ranked public universities in the country offer generous merit scholarships to lure top students from other states. At the University of South Carolina, for example, two-thirds of out-of-state freshmen receive scholarships starting at more than $9,000 a year. Top students, with high GPAs and SAT scores over 1500, often get full-tuition scholarships.

Strong students can likewise get a great deal at Ohio State University where two thirds of out-of-state students get the $44,000 annual price tag reduced to an average cost of less than $29,000. A similar scenario exists at Miami University in Ohio where two thirds of out-of-state students get the $49,000 annual cost reduced to $35,000. Other national public universities that lower their price tag for academically impressive out-of-state students include: The University of Michigan, Penn State, Iowa State and Oklahoma State universities, and the universities of Kansas and Iowa.

A handful of elite pubic colleges also offer need-based grants. The University of Michigan says it covers the full demonstrated financial need for out-of-state students from families earning up to $90,000. Of course, all of these grants are competitive and are typically awarded to students in the top 25% of the applicant pool with SAT scores over 1300.

For students who are not so anxious to spread their wings, there are plenty of great educational options at the eleven public colleges and universities in New Jersey. Rutgers is a highly ranked national university with 45,000 students, and hundreds of majors, at three campuses in New Brunswick, Newark and Camden. The College of New Jersey, with a scenic campus in Ewing, ranks third among regional universities in the north.

The nine other state schools, where students can frequently commute from home and eliminate expensive room and board costs, are: Kean, Montclair State, New Jersey City, Rowan, Stockton, Thomas Edison State, and William Paterson universities, New Jersey Institute of Technology and Ramapo College of New Jersey.

It's no secret that attending a public university is typically the most cost-effective way to get a college degree. But a recent study by *PayScale* noted that many of the public universities also offered the greatest likelihood of a high-paying career. Those that topped the list included Maritime Colleges, Military Academies and Technology Institutes.

The best public university in the country -- based on salary potential -- is a stone's throw from Yankee Stadium, according to PayScale statistics. It's the SUNY (State University of New York) Maritime College in the Bronx. With an in-state annual tuition of $6,470, and an out-of-state annual tuition of $16,320, it's about as affordable as a student can hope for. Its 1,600 students can anticipate the highest median income in both early career and mid-career salaries. Part of the reason for this success is its program offerings in fields such as: Naval Architecture, Electrical, Marine or Mechanical Engineering, Marine Transportation, Marine Environmental Science, Marine Operations and Maritime Studies.

Military Academies took 2nd, 3rd and 4th place in career salary potential, which is especially impressive since tuition is free! The United States Naval Academy at Annapolis (Maryland), The United States Military Academy at West Point (New York), and the United States Air Force Academy (Colorado) respectively topped the list. The Virginia Military Institute came in 7th place in the rankings.

Predictably, public universities that graduate a large percentage of STEM (science, technology, engineering and math) majors tend to have alumni with high earning potential. These students graduate with skills that are immediately in high demand. This accounts for Georgia Institute of Technology coming is 6th place, Colorado School of Mines earning 8th place, and the New Jersey Institute of Technology (NJIT) ranking 12th in this nationwide ranking.

Other colleges that earned high honors include the University of California at Berkley (5th place), the

Massachusetts Maritime Academy (9th place), and the University of California at San Diego (10th place). Students with a talent and love for math and science have some great college options to consider.

In addition to choosing a great college that offers their major of choice, another consideration for many college-bound students is location. It's wise for students to think ahead to the city in which they ultimately hope to live and work, and consider attending a college in that locale. Students make lifelong friends in college and connect to prospective employers through internships and their college's career services department. So it's wise to consider colleges in appealing cities that also offer great job prospects.

Two top cities for job seekers, according to the career site *Indeed*, are currently Miami and Orlando, Florida. *Indeed* considered the 50 metropolitan areas with the greatest number of job postings, and evaluated them on four factors: work/life balance, salary compared to cost of living, job availability and job security. The vast majority of the 25 "best places" for job seekers, according to *Indeed*, are warm weather cities. Two additional Florida cities made the list: Jacksonville and Tampa. So, too, did six California cities: Sacramento, San Jose, San Diego, San Francisco, Riverside and Los Angeles. Raleigh and Charlotte, NC, Memphis, TN, Las Vegas, NV, Atlanta, GA, and the Texas cities of Austin, Houston, and San Antonio were also recommended for their great job prospects.

Good news for students is that the average starting pay for new college grads is historically high -- hovering around $50,000. Of course, the salaries college graduates can expect is largely dependent on their field of study. Jobs in the STEM fields have starting salaries that are well above the national average. Topping the pay scale are software developers, engineers, and actuaries. Additional fields with high starting salaries are physicians in all specialties, lawyers, pharmacists, and financial managers. At the lower end of the pay spectrum for college graduates are jobs in animal science, social work, culinary arts, and parks, recreation and leisure studies.

Students who have not yet chosen their path of higher education would do well to take these "statistics" into consideration. If a future career in the Sun Belt is appealing, the easiest route is often to attend a college or university in a warm weather city with great job prospects. Students frequently convert college internships into full time jobs. College students also develop lifelong friends and prospective job contacts during their college days, so it's not a bad idea to start out in a city where you would like to stay.

On the other hand, some students see their college days as an opportunity to explore the world. From a financial standpoint, there are several advantages for students to seek a college degree abroad. It's hard to beat the price tag of Europe's public universities, which are largely free in Germany, Norway, France and Austria. As an added perk, health care is often fully covered and housing aid is available. In some other countries, including Turkey, Thailand, Brazil, and Iceland, college is either free or less than $7,000 a year.

Students willing to pay a bit more (between $7,000 and $13,000 a year) sometimes opt to attend one of 42 universities in the Netherlands. There, they find a choice of 300 English language undergraduate degree programs.

Prestigious universities in the United Kingdom and Australia may exceed $20,000 a year in tuition. But the fact that diplomas are earned in three years in the United Kingdom and for many programs in Australia still makes these international colleges a bargain by typical U.S. college price tags.

Also popular with American students, and just a short flight from many U.S. cities, is Canada. According to the latest statistics, there are more than 8,000 American students enrolled in Canadian universities. The most popular, McGill University in Montreal, offers students the opportunity to enjoy a vibrant bi-lingual city (French/English) while getting a world-class education. And American students don't have to cross an ocean to head home for the holidays!

The "best college for your money" is, of course, a different one for each student. The key for college-bound students is to carefully consider what they are seeking in a college education, and then identify those colleges and universities that are the best match within the financial constraints that will not leave them drowning in debt once their college days are a fond memory.

Importance of the FAFSA & Scholarship Tips

According to The College Board, about two-thirds of full-time students pay for college with the help of financial aid in the form of grants and scholarships. In order to be considered for most scholarships and loans, students need to file a FAFSA (Free Application for Federal Student Aid) anytime after October 1st of their senior year. It's best for families to file as soon as possible after October 1st as some colleges have early grant deadlines and some distribute aid on a first-come, first-served basis. As expected, the FAFSA asks many questions regarding money – both on the part of the students and their parents. These questions focus on income, savings, expenses, assets and liabilities.

The FAFSA form requests tax information from the prior year, so families can link their previously filed tax information onto the FAFSA form. For example, families of high school seniors can file a FAFSA in October of 2018 for the 2019-20 school year using data from their 2017 taxes that were, most likely, filed months before.

One question on the FAFSA is whether or not the student would like to be approved for Work Study. It's always wise for parents/students to answer "yes" to this question, as the student will then be eligible for work-related opportunities on campus. For example, if a college professor offers a student the opportunity to do paid research for him/her, the student would not be able to do so if not approved for Work Study. So it's always best to leave all options open. No one will ever force a student to take on a Work Study job, but it's best to be able to do so if the ideal job presents itself.

In addition to filing a FAFSA, students should do everything in their power to identify, and apply for, appropriate scholarships. The best way to go through college is debt free. The fewer the loans a student takes out, the less money – with interest – a student will have to pay back. Often students are awarded scholarships in their college acceptance letters. But that's only the tip of the iceberg, as few students are offered enough money to cover tuition, fees, room, and board at their college of choice. How do students cover the gap between what they are offered and what they actually need? The answer, too frequently, is student loans. Then, after graduation, students find themselves joining the work force in an entry-level job, with the expenses of living on their own, and with college debt that will take a decade or more to repay.

What students need to do is seek as many scholarships as they can find before beginning their college journey. The best place to start is in their high school guidance office where most local scholarship applications are filed. For example, scholarships are often offered by such groups as the Rotary Club, Elks, PBA, Home & School Associations, Education Foundations, Women's Clubs, Dukes Pop Warner, and both Democratic and Republican organizations. Although the awards may be on the smaller side -- between $500 and $5,000 -- the competition is limited to local, graduating students.

National scholarships, such as those offered by Discover Card, Toyota, Coca-Cola, McDonald's, Target, KFC, Kodak and Best Buy, offer scholarships that are much larger in scope, typically ranging from $10,000 to $20,000 a year. But just as the size of these scholarships is greater, so too is the competition. Tens of thousands of students nationwide seek these jackpots that are ultimately awarded to just a handful of students.

The more time and effort a student puts into the scholarship search, the better the chance for success. Scholarships that require essays of over 1,000 words, or a video or other project, typically have a much smaller applicant pool. So students shouldn't back away from those competitions that require some effort on their part.

Students should also seek scholarships from organizations with which they or their parents are personally affiliated. They might start with their church, temple, or other place of worship. If they are athletes, boy scouts or girl scouts, members of 4-H, or any other particular organization, they may be eligible for a scholarship. Parents, likewise, should check if their employer has scholarship money available. Families should also research scholarships for students of a particular ethnicity, as well as those for students seeking education for a particular career.

Another effective way for students to identify potential scholarships that are both appropriate and available – as fans of the ABC-TV hit show "Shark Tank" know – is to go to www.myscholly.com or the Apple App Store or Google Play Store where you can download the application for "Scholly: Scholarship Search." The cost is $2.99 on their website or 99 cents for a mobile download. Scholarship-seekers are asked a question in each of eight categories: gender, state of residence, current grade, grade point average, whether they are seeking merit or need-based aid, race, college major, and "miscellaneous" where there is an opportunity to identify such diverse characteristics as being an athlete, vegetarian, child of a veteran, or individual with ADHD or a learning or physical disability. The site, within five minutes, connects a user with a current list of available scholarships for which he/she a good match. According to Christopher Gray, a recent graduate of Drexel University who developed Scholly during his scholarship search, more than $1.3 billion of available scholarship money goes unclaimed each year. College-bound students may want to seek a piece of the pie!

ABOUT THE AUTHOR

Susan Alaimo, of Hillsborough, NJ, is the founder and director of SAT Smart. She holds a Masters Degree from Columbia University and, for the past 25 years, has successfully prepared thousands of New Jersey students for the PSAT, SAT, ACT, Subject Tests, AP courses and all high school subjects. Susan is an expert on the college application process, and has helped thousands of local students gain acceptance to the nation's most elite colleges and universities. Susan is a former college professor and college admission counselor, and is a longtime member of the New Jersey Association of College Admission Counseling.
Visit www.SATsmart.com

Made in the USA
Middletown, DE
03 July 2020